W9-CHS-142

High Impact Living

High Impact Living

A Guide to Total Achievement

by
BILL BROOKS

Price/Stern/Sloan Publishers, Inc.
1987

The excerpt from GET THE BEST FROM YOUR-SELF: The Complete System of Personal and Professional Development, by Nido Qubein © 1983 is reprinted with permission of Prentice-Hall, Inc., Englewood Cliffs, New Jersey.

The CREATIVITY KILLERS is excerpted from THE CREATIVE PROCESS, edited by Angelo Biondi © 1986, and is reprinted with permission of DOK Publishers, East Aurora, New York.

Copyright © 1987 by William T. Brooks
Published by Price/Stern/Sloan Publishers, Inc.
360 North La Cienega Boulevard, Los Angeles,
California 90048

Printed in the United States of America. All rights reserved. No part of this book may be reproduced, stored in a retrieval system or transmitted, in any form or by any means, electronic, mechanical, photocopying, recording or otherwise, without the prior written permission of the publishers.

ISBN: 0-8431-1787-7

This book is dedicated to my parents, Angela and the late Clifford Brooks, who taught me the value of integrity and commitment; to Jim Combs, my high school football coach, and first role model, who taught me discipline, drive, preparedness, and pride; to Father Edmund G. Ryan, S. J., who gave me the confidence to be myself; and to my mentor, Ron Willingham, who taught me who I really am. But most of all, I dedicate this work to my wife, Nancy, the brightest, most selfless and understanding person in the world. She is the mother of our two boys, Will and Jeb, who are the lights of my life and the breath of my soul. I have learned from these three the greatest lesson of all: to love and be loved unconditionally. Nancy, Will, and Jeb, I love you more than life itself.

TABLE OF CONTENTS

Introduction

Introduction

Sometimes it seems that change is the only constant element in our lives. Life's constant changes—a new job, moving to a new residence, disrupted relationships—can make your head spin. Too many changes, too massive in scope, coming too quickly, can leave you confused about:

- who you are.
- what really matters to you.
- what to do next.
- how it all fits.

Yet, in the midst of all the changes we go through, most of us feel a strong desire to make our presence felt wherever we find ourselves.

We want people:

- to pay attention to us.
- to care about what we think and feel.
- to listen to what we have to say.
- to respond to our needs and desires.

We want our lives to matter. We want to have an *impact* on the world around us. And, the more ambitious we are, the greater our desire to make our *impact* felt.

In fact, we often determine our effectiveness as human beings by how much impact we have. The real winners in each unique corner of the world are said to have high impact. What makes them winners is not that all the change has no effect on them, but that they are able to adapt to each new situation, and to influence the changes as they occur.

Somehow the winners always seem to rise above the turmoil and make things happen. They seem to get things done, to get others to do things effectively, and to make you glad they are around.

That's *High Impact Living*, and attaining that personal goal is what this book is about. We're going to explore what high impact is, what kinds of people have it, how they get it, and what they do with it.

We'll examine a philosophy of living that will enable you to think through how your life got the way it is and how you'd like it to be. But primarily this is a hands-on book of practical insights about how to make *your own ideas* become realities.

Unlike the pop psychology books which have become so popular during the last decade *High Impact Living* deals with your life as a part of the human race. Instead of taking the "micro-view" of life which suggests you "drop out and do your own thing," it takes a "macro-view," and suggests ways to make your life richer by finding your own place in the real world.

Is that the kind of person you are or want to be—a high impact person? Maybe you've always felt there is more to you than you've yet discovered or revealed to the world. Something inside you whispers (no matter how confusing and discouraging life gets) that you've got what it takes to be a real winner in the game of life.

That little voice inside is right. You really are unique. You were born something special. All your life experiences have shaped your individuality, and every person or group you've interacted with has added a new dimension to your uniqueness.

This book was written to help you sort through all the ways other people and events have impacted on your life, and how you can utilize all you've gained from those experiences and encounters to impact more forcefully on the lives of those around you.

I invite you to join me in a continuing search to discover exciting new ways to become a more effective and powerful person.

We start by taking a hard look at how our views of success have shaped our attitudes and actions. Next, we'll explore more productive ways of thinking and acting to increase our impact. Then we'll examine the skills required to impact forcefully on other people, and how to develop those skills. Finally, we will look at ways of dealing with the tension and stress of daily life and the pressure of constant change.

Applying the Lessons of Life

The philosophy of *High Impact Living* grew out of my own experiences with subcultures, as well as my educational background in sociology and anthropology.

It started when I was a boy of four or five, watching my parents re-direct the dead-end lives of youngsters in a boys' club they'd founded. It began to take shape as I looked over the shoulder of a gorgeous girl I was dancing with at a high school dance and saw a guy who never danced, standing alone and sad. I promised myself I'd do something to help people learn how to win at the game of life.

Many of these ideas were born as I struggled through the transition from being a high school football star to being a nobody fighting to stay in college. They matured during my experiences quelling riots and teaching cultural relations in Okinawa during the Viet Nam war, working with students as a college dean, and in more than fourteen years as a successful college football coach.

Now I spend my time speaking to large groups and leading seminars on personal development, sales techniques and human relations. As a professional speaker and trainer, I've learned more than ever how to make the most of what the people who surround me have to offer.

LET'S MAKE A DEAL

If this book is to be worth the time and energy you invest in it you I will have to work together.

I'll promise at the outset not to give you a lot of high-sounding philosophies that vanish when they're exposed to the realities of life. Everything you'll read here has been tested and proven in the laboratory of my own life. These ideas and techniques have worked for me, and I'm sure they will work for you.

I've ended each chapter with some suggested action steps to enable you to incorporate the ideas into your own life and help make the philosophy concrete.

Your task may be a little harder. To really get the benefits the book offers you'll have to ask yourself a lot of questions, some of them painful. You'll need to search out your own values, re-evaluate your most basic assumptions about life, and apply what you learn to your own experience. If you make the commitment to work on the exercises at each chapter's end you'll enrich your experience and deepen your understanding of how this material applies to you and how it can have an impact on your future.

And so, let us begin!

SECTION I

REDEFINING SUCCESS

CHAPTER ONE

Don't Conform . . . Adapt!

You never outgrow peer pressure. The pressure to conform starts in the cradle. At first, you're clearly in charge: you cry and someone pops a bottle in your mouth, rocks you to sleep or gives you a nice dry diaper. By the time you're a few weeks old you learn how to get the big faces that surround you to smile back at you.

Gradually, you learn there are certain things you can do to make the big people in your life respond with delight. Take your first shaky step and they say you're "a big boy" or "a big girl." Mutter a few semi-intelligible syllables and they go wild with glee. Learn to make your deposits in a potty instead of a diaper and they lavish praise upon you.

In kindergarten you begin to discover another whole group you can get to warm up to you—the other little people who surround you. They'll like you if you do and say certain things, and they will be very upset if you don't.

It's called socialization, and it means that you are learning to fulfill your need for love and acceptance by going along with the attitudes and practices of your "subculture," your own particular group within society.

By the time you hit high school you've really caught on to the game. You've learned that to be accepted by the people who surround you there are certain things you must wear and not wear, various words and phrases that carry special meanings, and specific actions that are either "cool" or not so "cool."

CONFORMITY HAS ITS PROBLEMS

Somewhere in adolescence you begin to notice there are some real problems with all this living up to the values and expectations of your subculture.

1. There are conflicts between various groups.

The expectations of the people your own age are different from those of the grown-ups you want to impress. Even among people your own age there are pronounced differences in values and acceptable actions.

Pretty soon you discover that there are winners and losers in the game of socialization. The winners all seem to huddle together, and the losers form their own groups. And there are other subcultures such as the "haves" and the "have-nots," the "achievers" and the "non-achievers," the "jocks" and the "brains," etc., etc., etc.

You find that your values are being shaped more and more by the group in which you feel most accepted.

2. The expectations of the groups are always changing.

A word that was "cool" yesterday is suddenly a relic of the past. Clothes you bought a few weeks ago no longer fit the group's norms. You go to a place where the gang always hangs out and discover it's been abandoned.

It becomes increasingly hard to make plans because the ground rules are always changing. You're never really sure you're in step with the ever-changing drumbeat.

3. Certain people set the pace, and others follow.

Nobody seems to know exactly why, but a handful of people set directions for everybody in the group. One kid laughs and everybody else laughs. Another person laughs and everybody looks at him as if he's crazy. One kid wears something new and the next day all the kids are wearing it. But let someone who isn't "in" try to set a new fashion and see if anyone follows suit.

Maybe you don't like the way the leaders do things, but you dare not break from the expectations of the group. Perhaps you are one of the leaders and you can't understand why people in other groups don't give you the respect you deserve.

4. It becomes harder and harder to be your own person.

All this is happening at a time when you are trying desperately to find out who you are. Feelings struggle within you, but you dare not express them openly for fear of being rejected. Hopes and dreams gradually take on more and more of the expectations and values of the group that matters most to you.

You have the nagging feeling that you could be more than the group will allow you to be, but you dare not risk finding out. You want to go out and slay the dragons, but you find that about all you can manage is an occasional campaign against a lizard.

5. You're constantly being shoved from one group to another.

You graduate from high school and suddenly find yourself thrust into a whole new subculture at college. You finish school and find that most of the expectations and values of students don't fit in the work environment. You get promoted and find you don't quite fit with either the executives or your co-workers.

You'd Rebel, But . . .

As you look around, you see a few people who don't seem to be quite as addicted to subcultures as you are. They seem to know who they are and where they're going, and don't really care what others think about them.

About the time you begin to find the idea of rebelling against your subculture appealing, you notice some rather disquieting things about the rebels. You notice they're not quite as self-assured as they seemed at first. Many of them are lonely, insecure and afraid. It's scary business to break away from the herd and become your own person.

Second, you notice that they are not loners as much as you had thought them to be. They've gravitated toward other, less obvious, subcultures that may even be more demanding than the ones they've left.

Third, you've started gaining a little ground in your own subculture and it doesn't seem quite so limiting for now.

You decide to wait awhile to make your great escape and become your own person. You invest more and more of yourself in your subculture, and gradually conform more and more to its expectations.

THE TRAP

One day it dawns on you that you've become "conservative." Conservatives are people who have invested so much of themselves in a subculture that they dare not risk anything that might jeopardize their investment. You realize that your personal values are in conflict with the values of your subculture, but you don't dare risk trying to act the way you really feel.

Yet something deep inside you whispers that you'll never truly be happy until you do start acting in ways that are consistent with the way you see yourself.

Maybe you try the escape route to ease the pain and frustration. You work a little harder than ever, you drink more and more or you spend more and more time in front of the boob tube. But you gradually realize that the monkey is not chasing you; he's on your own back.

The problem is that you can't resign from the human race. You are a part of society, and society is made up of subcultures. Whether you like it or not, you are involved in humankind, and always will be. Even those who escape to the wilderness find themselves coming back to buy and sell, to get help and to ease their pains of loneliness.

So what can you do? How can you be your own person, without exiling yourself from the people you love and need so desperately?

DON'T CONFORM—ADAPT

To conform is to *take the shape of* your subculture; to let *it* shape all your values, attitudes and actions.

There is another way to relate to your subculture—adapt. To adapt is to *adjust as necessary without losing your essential identity*. You learn how to play the game to win, how to balance your own values against the conflicting values of your subculture.

Perhaps that sounds like a formula for stress. In a way it can be. But tension is not all bad. In fact, everything that makes music, including the human voice, is under tension. When a violin string is tight enough to sound its purest note it is half-a-turn away from snapping from the pressure.

THINK IT THROUGH

Describe an incident or experience in which you experienced the problems of conformity in each of the following ways:

1. You were caught in a conflict between the values and expectations of two different groups to which you belonged:

_____

_____

2. You were in conflict with a new set of values that were emerging in some group to which you belonged:

_____

_____

3. You noticed that one or two people set the pace, and others in a group always followed them:

_____

_____

4. You felt more and more as if you were being squeezed into someone else's mold:

_____

_____

5. You found yourself thrust into a new group where expectations of you were significantly different:

_____

_____

ACTION STEP

As you review the situations above, decide whether you coped by conforming or adapting. Set a goal for shifting from conformity to adapting in each of the major areas of your present life.

CHAPTER TWO

Understanding Your Self-Image

Your eyes are the most revealing part of your personality, yet this window to your innermost being is closed to you.

For example, have you ever noticed that you cannot follow the movement of your own eyes as you look into a mirror? The slightest movement and the focal point shifts.

Others can see the anger, joy or pain in your eyes, but the best any of us can do is catch a fleeting glimpse of our own personhood in a mirror.

In the same way, we cannot see our own emotions, our attitudes or our values. Most of the time, we can only see the *results* of our actions rather than seeing our actions and movements.

Because of this inability to see ourselves in motion,

we must look to others to help us form our self-image—our own mental picture of ourselves.

Thus, more than most of us realize, our self-image is shaped by our subcultures. And, since our self-image shapes our attitudes and actions, we think and act according to the expectations of those groups.

This chapter is designed to enable you to focus on how your life has been and is being influenced by the many subcultures that have helped to shape your attitudes, expectations and actions. The better you understand how subcultures impact upon what you think and do, the better equipped you'll be to overcome their negative impact, build upon their positive impact and seek out those subcultures that bring out your best.

I. LIVING WITH SUBCULTURES

When I fly into a major city like Chicago or Atlanta, I'm always struck by how many people are gathered in such a small place. Everywhere you look, there's somebody—or a whole bunch of somebodies.

Grab a taxi and hit the expressway and you see tens of thousands of cars, trucks, campers, bicycles and buses carrying hundreds of thousands of people. They're all rushing like mad to get from somewhere to somewhere else.

All those people have come from a place they call home, and they're headed for other places where they work, learn, play or worship. They all seem to know where they're going, and you can only hope your cab driver knows where you're going.

Welcome to the world of subcultures; the microcosms that make up the larger society in which we all live.

Identifying Subcultures

Each group has its own symbols, values, language, practices and a code of expectations for each of its members.

Native Americans of two centuries ago rallied around totem poles, identified themselves by distinctive markings and clothing, and had strong tribal values. So strong were those values that young braves would dream of the day they could decorate their faces with warpaint and ride off to risk life and limb to defend them.

Of course, in what Marshall McLuhan called the "global village," many people believe we've outgrown such subcultures; that they simply don't exist anymore. In the American "melting pot," so the theory goes, the mass media have made us one great big family of human beings.

You need look no further than the news media themselves to see that subcultures are still very much a part of our society, and that they are shaping our lives in very powerful ways. With every major disaster or news story, the media invest great amounts of time and space getting reactions from people who view it differently depending on their subculture.

None of us can relate to the population of the whole world at once. We want to talk to people, to care about people and to matter to them. So we cluster in groups and find our identities among them.

II. THE POWER OF SUBCULTURES

Two athletes stand out in memory from the days when I was coaching football teams. Both were from poor and socially deprived backgrounds. But, both were bright and ambitious, good athletes and doing very well.

Yet, on separate occasions, they each came to me in tears and told me essentially the same thing. They were being ostracized from their home communities because they were acting and talking more and more like college kids.

The problem was that each of them was studying English grammar, making good grades and getting recognition from their new subculture for their achievements. So the subcultures from which they had come sought to enforce the old values. It seemed clear to them that they would either have to quit school, or live without the support of the communities they'd come from.

Despite my best efforts to encourage them to keep going, growing and learning, one of them eventually dropped out and went back to his community. I've often wondered what happened to him. I knew that, having tasted of the values of an achieving subculture, he would probably never feel comfortable with the values and expectations of his old group.

The other guy decided to tough it out and stay in school. He did very well, both in sports and in his studies. Later, he moved into a promising career and has done remarkably well at it. Yet, to this day, he still lives with the weight of his original subculture. No matter where he goes or how much he achieves, there will always be the nagging feeling of loss from being rejected by his community.

Of course, those are extreme examples. Yet each of us has felt pressure as we move from one subculture to another. The values and expectations of people who matter to us pull at us with an amazing force.

Equality and Other Myths

The pull of subcultures to enforce their values and expectations when we try to leave them is not the only pressure they exert. The inner workings of our groups also create enormous pressures as we struggle for our identities within them.

One of the strongest ideas in the American way of life is that "all men are created equal." But it doesn't take much experience with the real world to know how little influence this idea has on our actual experience.

Two people can be born into the same subculture, have the same opportunities, and share many of the same experiences, yet one of them will excel, while the other goes nowhere. Why? I don't think there is a simple answer to that question.

I do think, however, that a lot of it has to be traced to the inner workings of subcultures. For some strange reason, some people are tapped by the group early in life to be the stars and others are identified as the losers. But the masses of people are slated to live out their lives in the vast middle ground between winning and losing.

Part of the answer has to lie in the old idea of "tribal dominance"; the fact that for every chief there must be a whole bunch of Indians. There seems to be ample evidence that some people are born with that special something that causes them to move to the head of the pack. It can even follow them from one subculture to another.

Yet there is equal evidence that some people who are born to be nobodies learn how to play the game and become somebodies.

The Pressure of Multiple Groups

All of us constantly find ourselves involved with several different subcultures. We are members of families, social peer groups, groups of co-workers; we may also belong to special interest groups such as religious groups, clubs and sports teams.

The problem this poses is that each group exerts its unique pressures upon us to conform to its values and expectations. Since those values and expectations are often in direct conflict with each other, we feel torn between them. The pressure can be overwhelming.

If, for example, your career expectations call for extensive travel, but your family values insist you be home each night, you will constantly be torn between the two. Or if you grew up in a subculture with a strong work ethic and your peers put a high premium on recreation, you may find yourself approaching play as if it were work.

III. UNDERSTANDING HOW SUBCULTURES HAVE SHAPED YOUR LIFE

What happens is that we adopt many of the values and expectations of each subculture we are in, and carry some of them with us wherever we go and whatever we do.

When I was about four or five years old, my parents started a boys' club. My earliest memories are of my dad coaching Little League baseball, and my mom taking care of the field and chauffeuring people around.

Growing up in that subculture, I picked up some pretty strong values and expectations, which are still a part of my life today:

1. I was taught the value of teamwork and to this day consider myself a strong team player in any group.
2. I learned the value of hard work to get ahead.
3. I learned the importance of studying and thinking as a way of overcoming obstacles and problems.
4. I picked up a strong empathy for people who are struggling against tremendous odds, and have a great desire to help them.
5. I learned the value of setting high goals for myself and committing myself to reach those goals.

There are many other values I picked up along the way, but you get the idea.

You Never Start Even

You can move to a new city where no one knows you, take a new job, form all new relationships, start a whole new set of hobbies and even have plastic surgery done on your face, but you can never completely start over. The reason is that each subculture you live in puts its stamp on your mind and your emotions (sometimes even your body), and the warmer your feelings toward that group the more indelible that stamp tends to be.

When I was coaching, I could see what a powerful impact subcultures had on each football player who went out for the team. I could see the values and expectations of all the people who'd ever coached him, of his family and community, and of his peer groups. I was constantly aware that his whole view of life had been conditioned by all the people who had come across his path.

Those who had played on winning teams in high school came in with great expectations and an understanding of teamwork. But those who had played on losing teams either tried to do it all themselves or gave up at the first discouragement.

I found that a person's attitude was the single most important ingredient in building a winner. If a player had speed and size, those were valuable assets. But given the choice of speed and size or a good attitude, I would always opt for the good attitude.

Building a team usually meant imparting new values and expectations to the players who made up that team. I spent about as much time talking about setting goals and believing in yourself as I did talking about the mechanics of football.

Many years later, as a trainer, consultant and motivator, I find that the same thing is just as essential. If anything, I think the need is more pronounced in adults because we have been exposed to so many more subcultures during our lives.

Everywhere I go I see people who are hobbled by the subcultures of their past. They may be executives, salespeople, office workers or line employees, but they are each also a collection of the subcultures they have encountered along the way. Their values and expectations of themselves and others have grown out of the many groups that have helped to shape their lives.

Positive Influences of Subcultures

Many of the subcultures we find ourselves in exert very positive influences on our lives. They help us to shape positive values, expectations and behavior patterns.

I got a good taste of just how those positive influences can work when I went to Gettysburg College. I figured that my best chances of playing football were in a small college, since I was too small to play for a major school.

However, I was in for a rude awakening when I got to the college's campus in Pennsylvania. I went from being a *somebody* in one subculture to being a *nobody* in another.

First the school released the College Board scores for all incoming football players. Mine were in the lower ten percent. In my high school it had not been considered cool to study too hard, so I'd loped along academically. I wasn't a bad student, but I had never taken my studies very seriously. At college it seemed everybody wore glasses and spent endless hours with the books. My fears about flunking out took an abrupt upturn.

Next, I went out for the freshman football team, only to discover I was once again over my head. A huge sophomore center snapped that ball and flattened me before I knew what was happening. To make matters worse, one of the coaches belittled me in front of all the other players and loudly predicted I'd never make the team.

I was discouraged. I had been a real hot shot in high school. I'd always made reasonable grades, been very popular, and even served as state governor for the "Hi-Y" club during my senior year. I'd also been a starting player on a football team that had gone undefeated three of my four years in high school.

Here I was an underachiever in a subculture that placed high expectations on all its members. All I wanted was out. I'd pretty well decided to quit school, but two very dramatic things happened.

First, I was sent to talk to Dean Ramsey "Buck" Jones, who really helped me turn things around by showing me that I *could* achieve, and that I would never be happy as an underachiever.

Second, I had joined a fraternity that placed strong emphasis on academic achievement. They operated on a "big brother" system and the guy assigned to me was Pat Noonan. He not only encouraged me, he insisted that I spend at least twenty hours studying for each test I was to take. I'd have to give him a detailed log of my time, showing how I'd spent my twenty hours.

As a result of that positive influence, I was able to turn things around. I made the dean's honor roll in most terms and maintained a high grade point average throughout college. What's more, I made the freshman football team and went on to play all four years of college.

Even now, I look back on the expectations of that subculture as one of the most powerful influences of my life. I learned from the people around me that winning is mostly mental, and that's helped me immeasurably in every aspect of my life.

Those who would have you throw off all the expectations of the people from your past are overlooking the very positive impact our subcultures have on us.

Negative Influences of Subcultures

But the other side of that coin is the negative impact our subcultures can have on us. They can impart self-limiting values, cause us to lose sight of our own personal values and create an enormous amount of false guilt within us.

For example, my status in high school as a popular athlete and student leader caused me to grossly exaggerate my importance. It was crushing to discover that, in a new subculture, I was a "nobody."

People who grow up in a subculture that places a high value on financial success or academic achievement might find themselves feeling like failures if they decide to become a missionary.

Dr. Albert Schweitzer's peers in Europe became quite concerned when he chose to give up his lucrative teaching post at a prestigious university to "waste his life among the heathen lepers" of Africa. They sent a delegation to try to dissuade him from his "foolhardy" pursuit. Yet it was his violation of the expectations of his subculture that later won him the Nobel Peace Prize.

Likewise, a person who grows up in an underachieving subculture may feel tremendous feelings of guilt if he or she starts becoming very successful in another group. If you are a person who grew up in poverty, you may find it hard to shake off the shackles of your past and become the real winner you are capable of becoming.

Since all of us are built differently, you may go in the opposite direction. Remembering how bad it was when you were so poor, you might work yourself to death and constantly worry about not having enough money—no matter how much of it you make.

IV. MAINTAINING YOUR INDIVIDUALITY WITHIN YOUR SUBCULTURES

Perhaps the greatest challenge of all is being your own person in the midst of all the subcultures that constantly surround you.

As you look to others to help you form your own self-image, you may develop some pretty negative distortions that can hold you back from being successful and even from enjoying your life.

The biggest problem with subcultures is that they tend to have a great leveling effect upon their members. They can make us look, act and think like everyone else in our group.

You see it reflected on a broad scale in mass programming for television. Since the name of the game is rating points, programs are aimed at the widest possible viewing audience. So we get shows that appeal to people with fifth-grade mentalities, middle-class values and very modest expectations of achievement. As a result, we've got masses of people who've been programmed to underachieve, to expect simple solutions to complex problems and to look to someone else to change their lives for them.

But the leveling effect becomes even more pronounced in smaller subcultures. Dress codes, language and other symbols are much more rigidly enforced. Values and expectations become much more dominant.

One of the things that intrigued me, while I was in the U.S. Army during the Vietnam war, was how important uniforms, military procedures and protocol were to the whole military structure. Individuality was discouraged because it is absolutely essential that soldiers all think and act alike in combat situations.

Of course, the members of the protest movements targeted this sameness as their symbol for much that was wrong in America. They burned draft cards, flags and other symbols of the military-industrial complex. Their central value was expressed as "do your own thing" or "be your own person."

Yet, there was a remarkable sameness about them. Their "love beads," their ponchos and long hair made them as recognizable as any soldier in his uniform. Their psychedelic drugs and hang-loose lifestyle expressed their values and expectations as eloquently as any military procedure.

All subcultures tend to crush individuality and breed a sameness in values, practices, symbols and expectations.

Being Your Own Person

Many would say that your only hope of becoming your own person is to disavow identification with any group, and go it alone. I doubt seriously that such a solitary lifestyle is possible and, even if it were possible, it would be an awfully lonely existence.

The answer to this conflict is to forge your own identity as a person in the midst of the subcultures that surround you. It's not easy, but it's possible.

To do that, three things are necessary:

1. You have to choose and live by your own values. "I hate labels," veteran news commentator Harry Reasoner used to say, "because they tend to lump you with people with whom you have only one thing in common." He was right on target.

It's always easier to let the group do your thinking

for you; to let others decide what really matters and doesn't matter in your life. But you can only be successful and happy when you start choosing your own values for yourself.

Just because you accept one (or a few) of the values of a subculture does not mean you have to be guided by all their values. For example, you don't have to join the army just because you want to "be all you can be!"

The important thing is for you to know clearly what you believe and are acting upon.

2. You have to forge your own self-expectations. When I was a kid, I came in third in every race I ran because everybody was convinced that there were two guys in my subculture who could outrun me. The problem was that I let the group's expectations of me become my own expectations, and I never was able to outrun those guys. I never found out if I could beat them because I never expected it of myself.

People will identify you very quickly and ascribe certain performance capabilities to you. As a result, you may underachieve and always feel rotten about yourself because you can never live up to their expectations. Or, even worse, you may consistently perform below your capabilities because you let the group determine what you're capable of doing.

When my college coach shouted out that I'd never make the team, I could have taken that as a law coming from an authority figure, and proved him right. Instead, with the help of two key people, I became dead set to prove him wrong.

Only *you* know what you are capable of doing. You have to set your own self-expectations if you want to be your own person.

3. You have to function in a manner that is consistent with the way you see yourself. I see people all the time who use the cop out saying, "everybody does it." If all the others where they work show up late, they show up late. If all the others cheat on their tax returns, they cheat. If all the others grumble about their unfulfilled lives, they grumble.

Perhaps this business of functioning in a manner inconsistent with the way we see ourselves explains why so many people hate their jobs. They're allowing others to decide for them where they fit and what they *ought* to be doing, rather than taking a deep look at their own self-image and choosing for themselves what they are going to do with their lives.

Life's real winners get things sorted out and concentrate on their own goals. They compete against themselves, not everybody else. They set their own goals. They determine their own quotas, often far above the bosses'. They concern themselves with the person who stares back at them from the mirror every morning.

THINK IT THROUGH

For each of the typical subcultures listed below, describe:

A. Two primary values of the group—one positive and one negative.

B. Two self-expectations you developed from your association with the group—one positive and one negative.

SUBCULTURE

PARENTS:

Primary positive value: _____

Primary negative value: _____

Positive self-expectation: _____

Negative self-expectation: _____

SCHOOL:

Primary positive value: _____

Primary negative value: _____

Positive self-expectation: _____

Negative self-expectation: _____

A BOSS:

Primary positive value: _____

Primary negative value: _____

Positive self-expectation: _____

Negative self-expectation: _____

RELIGIOUS GROUP:

Primary positive value: _____

Primary negative value: _____

Positive self-expectation: _____

Negative self-expectation: _____

CO-WORKERS:

Primary positive value: _____

Primary negative value: _____

Positive self-expectation: _____

Negative self-expectation: _____

CIVIC CLUB:

Primary positive value: _____

Primary negative value: _____

Positive self-expectation: _____

Negative self-expectation: _____

SOCIAL GROUP:

Primary positive value: _____

Primary negative value: _____

Positive self-expectation: _____

Negative self-expectation: _____

ACTION STEP

Isolate the three most important personal values you have and make a firm decision as to how you can live more consistently with them. Make it a solid commitment and begin immediately to act upon it.

CHAPTER THREE

Redefining Your Vision of Success

It's one thing to say you want to be successful or happy in life, but it's often quite another to have a clear vision of precisely what those terms mean to you.

As I've worked with thousands of people through my speaking and consulting profession, I've been surprised to discover how many of them have only a vague idea of what their values are, and how they formed their values. It is also surprising how many people are investing their lives in pursuits that don't really reflect their own values.

In this chapter, I want to enable you to connect with the values that drive you, to evaluate whether or not they are your true values, and to set a course for success based upon your own value system.

I. CONNECTING WITH YOUR OWN VALUES

The dictionary defines a value as "something (as a principle or quality) desirable." It also uses terms such as "prized," "cherished," "held in high esteem" and "rated highly in relation to other principles or qualities."

I would simply define a value as a quality you rate higher than other qualities. It's a principle you believe in and are acting upon.

William Faulkner once told a student, "I have found that the greatest help in meeting any problem with decency and self-respect and whatever courage is demanded is to know where you yourself stand. That is, to have in words what you believe and are acting from."

Unfortunately, most people simply don't know what they believe and are acting upon. People may say that making money is what matters more to them than anything in the world. Yet, if you mention to them that you hear there is a great deal of money to be made in drug trafficking, they'll do a quick back-pedal. They'll discover there is something they cherish considerably more than making money.

On the other extreme are people who say, "money means nothing to me." Yet they often spend most of their lives and invest their most creative energies trying to make all of it they can. Those who say they are not in their careers for the money, usually would change jobs quickly if the boss quit paying them.

The point is that values have to be balanced against each other and success defined in terms of your total value system. Otherwise, you will either not be able to give life your best efforts or not be satisfied with success when you get it.

Discovering How Your Values Were Formed

Tell me about the subcultures you've lived and worked in, and I can tell you a great deal about your values. Our values both shape and are shaped by our choices of subcultures.

"Birds of a feather flock together." There's a lot in that old saw. We tend to seek out those people and groups that value the same things we do.

For example, if one of your highest values is physical fitness, you probably spend a lot of time around gymnasiums or other athletic institutions because you like to be around other physical fitness buffs.

"Oh no!" you may protest, "I go there for the equipment!"

"Why don't you buy your own equipment?" I might ask.

"Can't afford it!" comes the terse reply.

Yet you could probably buy a pretty good gym system for the amount of money you have invested in your automobile—if you didn't like being around a physical fitness subculture. And, there's not a thing wrong with it. I'm simply noting how we tend to surround ourselves with people who believe and act the way we do. We choose those subcultures that reflect our values.

On the other hand, our values are shaped by the subcultures that surround us. Earlier, I pointed out that we often spend much of our time around people with whom we share only one (or at most a few) values.

For instance, some people detest the values of

people they work around everyday. They may try to get along with their co-workers, but when quitting time comes, they shoot out of the workplace like a bullet.

However, if we work around people long enough, we'll begin to find ourselves talking, thinking and even acting as they do.

Let me illustrate from my own experience. I don't think of myself as an "egghead" or an academe. As a football coach I never quite fit with the academic subculture. But, as a college administrator, I was always a little on the outside with other coaches.

I'm convinced that both of those subcultures had a lot to do with making my value system what it is today. My exposure to the academic environment probably had a great deal to do with the high value I now place on education, the way I talk and the way I conduct seminars. Likewise, my strong sense of teamwork and high achievement ethic probably were greatly enhanced by my experiences in the athletic subculture.

Lest I have people from both camps throwing rocks at me, I won't go into any of the negative values I picked up from either. But we all pick up both positive and negative values from all our subcultures as we go through life.

The big question is always: "Do your subcultures determine your values, or do they merely reflect your values?" On the surface that may appear to be an empty riddle, but if you look a little deeper you'll see that it is a very crucial question.

Are You an Affective or an Effective Person?

A leading psychologist observed that all of us have our affective and effective sides. Only one letter is different in the two words, but the difference in their meanings is great.

Our *effective* side is the part of us that *affects* other people; our *affective* side has to do with how much *we are affected* by other people. We all do a little of both—affecting and being affected by others—but with some of us one side is dominant.

The problem arises when we find ourselves living the way our subcultures have affected us rather than having an impact on the people who surround us. Then we are allowing others to choose for us what matters, what we believe and how we spend our time.

It's one thing to be influenced by your subculture in minor ways, such as picking up a local accent from living in a community for a long time. But when the influence is pervasive, as with picking up a sedentary lifestyle from people who sit around all the time, it can shape our lives against our own deeper values.

Life's real winners lean more to the effective side. They choose for themselves and they influence others more than they are influenced by them. So it's quite appropriate to ask if you are an affective or an effective person.

Connecting with Your Own Value System

I once read an oriental fable about a little tiger that was orphaned shortly after birth, and was raised by a friendly herd of goats. All day, every day, that little tiger played with the goat kids, drank milk from the nanny goat and slept in the goats' cave.

The problem was that the little fellow came to think of himself as a goat. He tried as hard as he could to bleat like a goat, to cultivate a taste for grass and paper and to play like any other goat. But, somehow, he never could quite make it.

One day, a huge Bengal tiger came bounding into the clearing where he was playing with the goats, and let out a gigantic roar. All the goats went scampering for cover but, for some strange reason, the little tiger felt drawn to this magnificent creature.

Finally, the big tiger led the little fellow down to a nearby brook and suggested he take a look at his reflection in the water. The little tiger was amazed! Then the big tiger sat back on his haunches and let out a roar that shook the jungle.

"There!" he said tauntingly, "Why don't you roar like that?"

The little tiger sat back and strained as hard as he could. Eventually, he felt a tiny rumble deep within his stomach. It grew stronger and stronger. At last, he opened his mouth wide and let out a jungle-shaking roar of his own. From that day forward, so the fable goes, he knew he could never again be a goat.

If I could say one thing to you in this book, it would be that you really are a tiger—not a goat! If I could inspire you to do one thing, it would be to connect with your own deepest values and never again settle to invest your life in anything less.

How to Connect With Your Own Value System

Of course that sounds simple enough, doesn't it? But I've found that many things that sound simple are not easy. It's simple to run a marathon, but it's not easy. It's simple to make a million dollars, but it's not easy. It's simple to break a negative habit, but it's not easy.

Connecting, and staying in touch, with your deepest personal values is a tough and continuous challenge. It involves serious thinking, asking yourself some hard questions and carefully analyzing your actions and attitudes. Yet it's the only way you can really know what values are driving you.

Before we take an in-depth look at how to do it, let me observe that most of us have two kinds of values—ideal values and actual values. Ideal values are the ones we'd like to be driven by: the idealized principles we'd like to think are the driving forces behind all our attitudes and actions. Our actual values are those principles that make us do things all day, every day. There is often a significant difference between the two.

To enable you to connect with your values—both ideal and actual—here's a list of questions I've found very helpful. I'll repeat them at the end of the chapter. Read through them for now, then search them through in-depth when you finish the chapter.

1. What is my personal definition of success? If I became very successful, what would my life be like? Ideal value? Actual value?
2. What three principles most frequently guide my decisions and actions? Ideally? Actually?
3. What three qualities do I consider most essential for reaching success (as I define success)?
4. What excites me more than anything else in the world? What is my greatest treasure?
5. What is my greatest fear in life?
6. What is my primary consideration in making decisions about: money? career? relationships? time allocations?
7. What percentage of my time is spent in direct and active pursuit of my ideal of success?

8. What priority do I place on the following areas of life: career, family, financial security, recreation, spiritual growth?
9. How would I like most to change my life?
10. What will my life be like ten years from now if I continue in my present directions?

II. UNDERSTANDING YOUR OWN VALUE SYSTEM

As you can see, those are relatively simple questions. They require some thought, and the more thought you put into them, the more productive they will be for you. But any reasonably intelligent person can answer any of them.

However, understanding what your answers mean to you may not be quite as easy.

For example, if your answer to the first question deals only with your career or money, what does that imply about the rest of your life? Defining success only in financial terms cannot possibly meet all your needs as a total human being.

Or consider what it means if some of your answers conflict with each other. For instance, if you define success primarily in terms of money, then (in question #8) rank your family at a higher priority level than your career, it suggests you have a conflict in ideal values and actual values.

Understanding your own values is both an event and a process. It is an event because it involves doing something in a deliberate way, at a specific moment. And it is a process because it is never quite finished. As your life changes, you will find your values changing.

Forging a Value System

Each of us has a value system, whether we recognize it or not. There is a set of guiding principles that we use as a basis for all our decisions and actions.

We either choose our own value system, or we allow the subcultures and circumstances in which we live to choose that value system for us.

Sadly, most people simply take life as it comes and allow all their value judgments to be made for them. They're a little like flounders. Flounders lie on the bottom of the ocean and soak up whatever comes floating by them. It makes little difference whether what comes floating by is good nourishing food or poisonous pollution. They just take it in and build their lives around it. Maybe you know some people like that.

But there are others who are more like trout. They know where they want to go and expend themselves in an effort to get there. If they have to swim against the tide or upstream, they'll do it to get where they want to go.

There are two techniques that can be helpful to you in forging your own value system. Both are based on William Faulkner's idea of knowing where you stand. You might want to choose one or the other; or you may prefer to use a blending of the two.

Value System Formulation Technique 1: Start by making a list of all the facets of your life you consider important and rank them by priorities. You should include things such as family life, career development, social development, physical fitness and mental/spiritual growth. Next, write out the two or three overriding principles that guide you in each area. Keep the list handy and constantly check your actions to make sure they are consistent with your value system.

Value System Formulation Technique 2:   Write out a simple, but complete, statement of the purpose of your life. It should be short enough to easily memorize, but complete enough to encompass every area of your life. Let that statement of your purpose become the value system through which everything you do and say is filtered.

Deciding Which Values to Keep And Which to Throw Out

A value is any principle, quality or thing we make a priority in our lives. Not all values are equal, some will be more important at various stages of our lives, and some are downright destructive to us.

Obviously, physical fitness is a value. Whatever we set out to do, we need to be in good enough shape to do it. Yet if we get so caught up in building a strong, slim, healthy body that we leave no time for our families, or our mental development, we can easily become so depressed we don't have the drive even to keep our bodies fit—much less do anything else.

The relative priority of certain values will change as we find ourselves in different circumstances of life. For example, developing financial security might be a relatively important priority for a young adult with a growing family. However, it would have little significance for a person who was being held indefinitely as a prisoner of war.

Some values are so idealized that they can be destructive to us. For instance, a person who places physical beauty at the top of his or her priority list is headed for a rude awakening. You may be able to postpone the wrinkles and crow's feet from your face for a while, but sooner or later age will catch up.

Some people live out their lives frustrated by their inability to actualize their idealized values. One way you can recognize them is that they always seem to be at war with themselves. They're torn between their ideal values and the actual conditions in which they live.

One key to living peacefully with yourself, and always being at your best, is to learn how to sort through your values to determine which ones to keep and which to throw out. Probably the best guidance I can give you about how to do it is found in the ancient prayer of St. Francis:

> "God grant me the serenity to accept
>   the things I cannot change,
> The courage to change
>   the things I can (and should) change,
> And the wisdom to know the difference."

Another approach you might find helpful is to keep asking yourself, "How much will this matter to me in ten years?"'

III. RE-STRUCTURING YOUR LIFE AROUND YOUR VALUES

We saw in chapter one that there are three things each of us must do to be our own person amid all the subcultures that surround us:

1. You have to choose and live by your own values.
2. You have to forge your own self-expectations.
3. You have to function in a manner consistent with the way you see yourself.

But how do you do all that? The answer is a little like the one given by the producer who was asked how he got a live cougar on top of the Lincoln/Mercury sign for a commercial. "Very carefully!" was his terse reply. Let's hope I can be a little more helpful than that.

The key to always keeping your life in tune with your own values is to constantly restructure your attitudes and actions around those values. Here are some clues to help you do that.

Restructuring Clue 1: Ultimately, You Decide

Each of us has only one true freedom in life, according to psychiatrist Victor Frankl. It is a freedom no one can give to us, and no one can take away. Each of us has the freedom to choose how we will react to whatever happens to us.

You cannot always determine what happens to you, but you can—and always do—choose how you will react to what comes along.

It means you cannot ultimately leave your choices about values, or actions based on those values, to some subculture. Ultimately, you decide what values will guide you and what you will do about them; even if your choice is to adopt the values and practices of one or more of your subcultures.

Restructuring Clue 2: Your Attitude Determines Your Actions

Tell me what you think, and I can tell you what you are most likely to do in almost any given situation. That's because our attitudes determine our actions.

After more than 2,500 years of philosophy, psychology and motivational research, no one has been able to come up with a better way to express the relationship between our actions and attitudes than the Hebrew king who said: "As he thinketh in his heart, so is he."

The fact is that you are your own person. If you don't like the sort of person you are, or are becoming, the place to start changing yourself is in your attitude about life.

Restructuring Clue 3: Your Actions Shape Your Life

Scapegoating is one of America's favorite sports. It seems easier to blame our circumstances, our parents or our subcultures for everything that's wrong in our lives than to face up to the fact that most of what is wrong is the result of our own actions.

If you are not living in harmony with your ideal values, don't waste your time trying to fix the blame. Expend your energies taking positive actions to change the situation.

Restructuring Clue 4: Your Emotions Are Symptoms—Not Guides

People who only do what they feel like doing are bound to spend the rest of their lives unable to do what they feel like doing. A part of maturing is coming to realize that your emotions cannot ultimately be used as a guide for your actions.

Emotions are valuable aids as signals to show how close to your ideals and values your actions are. Just as a doctor looks at symptoms, you can use them to determine if something is wrong, and even to discover what it is. But a clear thought is always superior to an emotion as a guide to actions.

Restructuring Clue 5: Restructuring Is a Life-Long Process

I've met many people who are trying to live out their lives by values they held when they were much younger. As a result, they are miserable in their present circumstances.

Take, for example, the successful professional athlete who remains a "jock" throughout his life. He values his trophies more than he values his goals. He spends most of his time talking about the way his life was, instead of facing the way it is and the way it can become.

The happiest people I know are the ones who always keep their values in harmony with the circumstances and subcultures they find themselves in at any given moment. They concentrate on what will get them what they want most out of life now, and for the future, not on the ideals they prized when things were different for them.

TYING IT ALL TOGETHER

You can only expect to become successful and happy in life when you have a clear understanding of what those terms mean to you; when you stay in constant touch with your own ideal values and keep your actions in harmony with them.

What does all this mean to you? Take some time to work through the following exercise. Plot a course to clarify your own values and bring your whole life in harmony with your own definition of success in every area of your life.

THINK IT THROUGH

Use the following questions as a guide to connect with your own personal values:

1. What is my personal definition of success? If I became very successful, what would my life be like?

Ideal value: _____

_____

Actual value: _____

_____

2. What three principles most frequently guide my decisions and actions?

Ideally: 1. _____

2. _____

3. _____

Actually: 1. _____

2. _____

3. _____

3. What three qualities do I consider most essential for reaching success (as I define success)?

1. _____

2. _____

3. _____

   4. What excites me more than anything else in the

world? _____

_____

   5. What is my greatest fear in life? _____

_____

   6. What is my primary consideration in making decisions about:

Money: _____

Career: _____

Relationships: _____

Time allocations: _____

   7. What percentage of my time is spent in direct and

active pursuit of my ideal of success? _____

_____

   8. What priority do I place on the following areas of

life: Career _____ , Family _____ , Financial security _____ ,

Recreation _____ , Spiritual growth _____ .

   9. How would I most like to change my life? _____

_____

10. What will my life be like ten years from now if I continue in my present direction? _____

_____

ACTION STEP

Plan and take a definite course of action for the immediate future that will lead you closer to bringing your attitudes and actions into complete harmony with your own definition of success.

CHAPTER FOUR

Creative Thinking and Innovative Action

"Choose your rut carefully; you'll be in it for the next forty miles." Living in subcultures can do that to us. They can lock us into set directions, keep us plodding along to avoid bogging down, hold us back from doing our best and ultimately determine our destination.

But it doesn't have to be that way. Creativity and innovation are the paths out of the rut and each of us has the creativity to break out and build whatever life we choose for ourselves.

That's what this chapter is all about—creative thinking and innovative action. Let's explore together what keeps us from being more creative, how to become more creative, and how to use our creative abilities to get more of what we want out of life.

Some Have It, and Some Don't?

Many people believe that creativity is something you're either born with or without. They speak of Einstein, Bach and da Vinci as "gifted people," and of their creative powers as "genius." "Some have it, and some don't," they'll tell you.

Of course, they're half right. There is ample scientific evidence that some people have an extraordinary ability to create, to organize data and to reason out complex issues. Some do seem to have a "natural eye for art," or an "uncanny knack with figures," or a "sixth sense about certain things."

But the other half of that truth is that all of us have far more creativity than we ever use. To create simply means "to produce through imaginative skills." All of us have an imagination, and skills can be developed through training and use.

"Throughout our lives we use only a fraction of our thinking ability," a brain specialist from the Soviet Union, Dr. Ivan Yefremov, once said. "We could, without any difficulty whatever, learn forty languages, memorize a set of encyclopedias from A to Z, and complete the required courses of dozens of colleges." Every major study done in America since that time has supported his conclusion.

That little voice in you that keeps whispering "There's more to you than you've realized!" is right. I'm not trying to convince you that you're another Thomas Edison, Dorothea Dix or Henry Ford. What I would love to do, however, is inspire you to become *yourself* multiplied by at least ten—maybe even by a hundred.

I. UNDERSTANDING OUR CREATIVITY BLOCKS

"If you're so darned smart, why ain't you rich?" It's a good question. If all of us are blessed with such overpowering mental capabilities, why do so many of us spend our whole lives operating at such a small percentage of our capacity?

When you were a little kid, creativity probably came pretty easily for you. You could sit and daydream for hours at a time. In your imagination you could fulfill all your fondest fantasies: see yourself flying without wings, slaying a dragon, commanding a huge army, receiving the adoration of all.

What happened to that imagination? Sadly, most of us outgrew it. You learned the truth about Santa Claus, Cinderella, G.I. Joe and the money tree. "Grow up!" adults told you. "It's time to face reality. Learn there's no free lunch."

Chances are pretty good that's exactly what you did. You put away your childish daydreaming and got on with putting foundations under your castles in the air.

Now that you're an adult you've begun to notice that your "castles" look more like log cabins. Play has given way to tedium. Perhaps your daydreams have become endless nightmares.

Imagine for a moment that your creativity is a giant river that starts high in the mountains. As it roars toward the sea it begins to pick up debris along the way; fallen trees, rocks, pollution, and algae. Its waters become thick and murky and don't flow as freely. Finally, all that debris piles up into a huge dam and your raging river is reduced to a tiny trickle.

That's precisely what happens to our creativity as we go through life, meeting obstacle after obstacle, moving through one subculture after another, and taking on more and more responsibility. These things become like dams bottling up our spontaneity.

Eventually we find ourselves using our high-powered imagination to sort through things such as what we're going to wear to work, how to improve our golf stroke or which television show to watch.

At least half the process of breaking through those blockades is understanding what they are. I want to help you identify some of the more common obstacles. Some or all of them may be keeping you from becoming the powerful person you know you were meant to be. I call them creativity dams.

Creativity Dam 1: Endless Routine

Some routine is necessary, even desirable, but a steady diet of it can dam up creativity like almost nothing else.

Paperwork is a minute example. We find ourselves shuffling endlessly through papers and mail, often looking at the same piece of paper five or ten times. After all, we reason, if it's written or printed it must be important. Besides, we've always done it that way.

I've discovered that I can cut my paperwork time by about two-thirds by simply eliminating everything that's not vital to my success, and taking action on each piece of paper the first time I see it.

It's not hard to look around in your life and discover many routines you go through for no good reason. You've simply done those things so often they've become habits. Incidentally, a habit is nothing more than an action you take so many times you can do it without thinking.

The problem with excessive and useless routines is that they breed tedium. Our minds become cluttered, listless and inert. We begin to suffer from a lack of mental stimulation and our thoughts settle into fixed patterns.

Eventually, we begin to think there is little we can do to change our lives, we become preoccupied with defending the status quo, and we readily accept defeats we would once have turned into victories.

Let me urge you to look constantly and carefully at all the routines of our life and develop the new habit of rooting them out before they seize your imagination and stifle your creativity.

Creativity Dam 2: Fatigue

Have you ever noticed how hard it is to create when you're exhausted? It's not that your mind gets tired, because your brain is not a muscle and is not subject to fatigue, according to scientists. The mechanisms that operate the brain, however, do get tired and eventually will quit operating properly—or stop altogether.

Fatigue produces a mental sluggishness, an "I just don't care" attitude. It can easily cause us to become irritable and waste a lot of creative energy lashing out at people or kicking the poor cat. Perhaps worst of all, fatigue breeds a feeling of hopelessness and the sense that we're going to keep on being tired of being tired.

Part of the solution, of course, is to make sure we always get enough sleep and physical rest. It's amazing how much more creative you feel after a good night's sleep.

But there are a couple of other factors that have a great deal to do with getting rid of the fatigue that is so devastating to creativity.

First, emotional fatigue can be even more destructive to spontaneity than physical fatigue. That's the kind of fatigue brought on by excessive stress and tension. It not only exhausts us, it hinders all efforts to relax and rest. We can get so caught up with the challenges and problems of life that we find ourselves struggling with the struggle itself.

It is extremely helpful to build into the incredibly hectic schedule ample time for diversion, for physical exercise, for simply letting off steam and having fun. I'm convinced that the runner's high we hear so much about comes largely from the mind's exhilaration at being set free from all the conflicting values and its enjoyment of concentrating on one simple task.

Second, creativity is an activity that requires its own investment of time and effort. It takes time and energy to create. Ideas are like seeds you drop into the ground; they have to germinate, sprout roots and grow up before they produce fruits.

People who only allocate the time for thinking and creating when they think they have nothing productive to do ought not to be surprised if nothing fresh springs from their thinking time.

If you want to really see your creativity flourish, and see your whole life take off in new directions, just try taking some of your most productive time every day to let your creative juices flow freely. You'll be amazed at what happens!

Creativity Dam 3: Negative Thinking

The optimist sees an opportunity in every problem. The pessimist sees a problem in every opportunity. Seeing yourself and your circumstances in a negative way can stifle any hope of applying your imagination to creatively solve the problems that plague you.

"But you don't understand," people often protest when they hear me say something like that, "my life really is difficult. . . . Everywhere I look, I see a huge problem."

Of course, life is difficult. It's difficult for everyone; even those who are born rich, who seem to have everything going for them, or who have the jobs you'd love to have. But life is also beautiful. It all depends on how you look at it.

Negative thinking puts your creativity in cold storage and breeds a narrow-minded view of everything around you.

For example, people in my time management seminars often tell me they hate coming in late for work everyday. They find it humiliating and embarrassing, a constant source of conflict with their bosses and co-workers.

Yet, when I ask them what they're going to do about it, they will answer, "There's nothing I can do. . . . It's just the way I am! I've always had a problem with being ten or fifteen minutes late."

The problem is that they've accepted the problem. By saying, "It's just the way I am!" they've closed off all possible creative approaches to a solution.

Interestingly, negative people tend to flock together and form subcultures of negativism. Moreover, we tend not to stop at saying there's no solution to our coming in late; we defend ourselves by saying, "I'm not the only one who comes in late." Then we seek out other people who have the same problem, and it becomes "us against them."

To compound the problem, the more you feed that negative attitude, the bigger it grows. One major concern can become a symbol for everything that's wrong in your life. Pretty soon, you begin to feel that nothing is right at work or at home.

"The greatest discovery of my generation is that a person can alter his life by altering his attitude of mind," said philosopher and psychologist William James.

A positive mental attitude can do wonders to stimulate creativity and get the imagination working again. The choice is always ours.

Creativity Dam 4: Fear

In the aftermath of the tragic loss of seven crew members in the explosion of space shuttle Challenger, the news media interviewed several famous test pilots including General Chuck Yeager. I was particularly captivated by his reply to a question from a reporter.

"When you discover that something has gone wrong," the reporter asked, "what do you do to keep from freezing up from panic?"

"You realize that you can't do anything to help your situation if you panic," he replied. "It's foolish to worry about what you cannot control . . . so you get busy doing whatever you can to solve the problem. . . . That way you at least give yourself a fighting chance."

It's easy to see how panic can cause our imaginations to shut down, but most of our day-to-day fears don't take the form of panic. They come to us as anxieties about some impending doom, worries about our future, or a nagging feeling that something is wrong.

Whatever form it takes, fear is a deadly enemy to creativity. Our most creative resources are drained off by our efforts to flee the most immediate danger we perceive.

General Yeager's philosophy about handling a panic situation holds some valuable clues about how to use your creativity to overcome fear, rather than being overcome by it.

Clue 1: Recognize that you can choose how you will react. You might not be able to control a given problem or situation, but you *can* control how you will react to it. Making a firm rational decision to deal with the problem, rather than running from it, is often the first step toward setting creative solutions in motion.

Clue 2: Realize that it is foolish to worry about things that are beyond your control. Worrying is like throwing a bucket of water on the tiny spark of creativity that glows deep inside. The greatest antidote to worry is a conscious decision not to worry, and a dogged determination to enforce that decision.

Clue 3: Get busy doing what you can to solve the problem. You'll be amazed at how many of the concerns you worry about will simply vanish when you get busy doing something constructive to change the situation.

Clue 4: Always look for the *serendipity* effect in solving any problem. Thomas Edison often said that the solutions to most of the problems he'd faced seldom involved new information. Usually, those solutions came from a new way of looking at information that was readily at hand.

Clue 5: Plan ahead to take full advantage of your solutions and avoid future problems.   The real movers and shakers in life always seem to look for the broader implications of their problems and solutions. When Alexander Graham Bell set about to solve his wife's deafness problem, he failed. As he worked on a primitive hearing aid, it began to occur to him that many people would find the device he invented instead quite useful. He never really solved his wife's hearing problem, but he invented the telephone and reshaped world communications by applying what he learned to other needs.

Life's real winners always see themselves not only solving the present crisis, but also laying the ground-work to avoid similar problems in the future. They don't want to waste their energies solving the same problem again and again. Perhaps that explains why winners always keep winning and losers always keep losing.

Creativity Dam 5: Scapegoating and Making Excuses

Some of us seem always to be saying "if only. . . ." If only we had been born taller or shorter, better look-ing, richer, a different race or sex, our lives would be so much better. No problem, it seems, is so great that it cannot be blamed on someone or something.

Scapegoating and making excuses stifles cre-ativity by shifting the responsibility for solutions away from us.

Great ideas have to incubate in creative minds if they are to grow up into useful activities. Many great ideas are killed by excuses before they have a chance to survive and grow. Consider these creativity killers from the Creative Education Foundation:

1. It won't work. In most cases, that reaction comes too quickly, with too little data to support it. How do you know it won't work until you've tried it?

2. Let's form a committee. This is an action-stalling suggestion from someone firmly committed to maintaining the status quo.

3. We've never done it before. Everything we do we once did for the first time.

4. It isn't in the budget. If it's a new idea, how could it be in the budget? Budgets usually represent yesterday's planning based on the facts of the day before.

5. It doesn't fit in with our policies. Policies should be guides to actions, not barriers to progress.

6. It's probably premature. The way that premature but good ideas get an opportunity to mature is through the discussion, work and testing of progressive-minded people.

7. Our business is different. All too often, business leaders think too narrowly and confine their sources of ideas to their own industries or companies. The best place to look for innovative ideas is outside your usual, routine sphere of influence.

8. We're doing okay without that. This is the battle cry of lazy, insecure people. Successful people are always striving for new ways to do even better. Besides, why settle for "doing okay," when you can be "doing great"?

9. The boss/our clients would never go for it. Don't be so sure. Very few people are really that good at mind-reading. You simply can't know if you don't ask.

10. We tried it, and it didn't work. Sometimes the best *new* idea is an old idea whose time has come. Small cars bombed when American manufacturers tried to sell them in the late forties and early fifties, but foreign manufacturers almost wiped out the American automobile industry with them two decades later.

II. SIGNPOSTS TO GREATER CREATIVITY

"I wish I had lived in your generation," a young assistant once lamented to Thomas Edison. "Everything worth inventing has already been invented."

"Young man," retorted the creative genius, "yours is the most exciting age of history. . . . You will see more inventions in your lifetime than I ever dreamed about."

History has proven that he was right. Experts say the total compendium of human knowledge is now doubling every ten years, and that more than ninety percent of all the scientists who ever lived are alive today.

But how do you become a creative thinker in the midst of so much negativism and with so many daily challenges? Here are some signposts to help point the way:

1. Develop and maintain a creative mindset. Creativity is, overall, a state of mind, an attitude, a mental alertness for better ways to do things. If you can just come up with and implement one new, good idea every day, you'll soon be miles ahead of the pack.

Negative thinking is a nasty, self-destructive habit. The best way to break a bad habit is to start a new good one. Practice thinking creatively until it becomes your natural response to any challenge you face.

2. Don't conform—adapt. Conformity and maintaining the status quo are the enemies of creativity. Don't let the world around you squeeze you into its own mold.

Instead of conforming, look for ways to adapt. Stay on the alert for ways to improve whatever circumstances you face.

3. Surround yourself with creative people. If negative attitudes are contagious, positive and creative attitudes are even more contagious. If you want to be successful, spend your time with successful people.

One of the most productive environments for new ideas is a brainstorming session. A group of creative people sit together and toss out all their ideas as they tackle some problem or objective, all negative and judgmental reactions are banned. Usually, in that creative atmosphere, several good ideas will emerge, the problem will be solved, and a plan to avoid the problem in future will be implemented.

4. Keep your mind uncluttered. Mental self-discipline is a great aid to creative thinking. Practice clearing your mind of all irrelevant concerns when you set out to think or when it's time to rest. You may need to get out of your work environment, or do something like read a book, take a walk or listen to music. Learn to clear away distractions and eliminate unnecessary interruptions.

Probably one of the greatest sources of mental clutter is procrastination. We put off a task we feel we should do, but we never really quite get it out of our minds. If we postpone enough tasks or decisions, we walk around with countless mental "to do" lists cluttering up our thoughts and find it hard to concentrate on anything. If it's worth putting on your list, do it now; if it's not, forget it.

5. Maintain a steady flow of input/output. Creativity requires good raw material to work with. A steady flow of new ideas can do wonders to stimulate your imagination.

That's why sales trainer extraordinaire Charles "Tremendous" Jones so strongly emphasizes that "leaders are readers." We're fortunate these days to have so many good books and articles being published. Biographies of great people, good motivational books, and periodicals provide a ready source of new ideas and new ways of looking at old information. You might find a speed reading course helpful.

I also think everyone can benefit greatly from one stimulating seminar per month. Our minds are like bodies of water, when they're in motion they stay fresh and vital; when they become still, they stagnate.

It's equally important to have regular outlets for your creativity. Writing things down helps you organize your ideas and develop them more fully. Expressing yourself through art, music or sports can also keep the brain in shape and ready for action.

6. Develop greater reasoning powers. Obviously, we all have enormous storage capacity in our brains—more capacity than we could ever use. However, one of the most important ways we access and utilize all that brainpower is by reasoning.

It is interesting to me to see how many creative and successful people enjoy games like chess, backgammon, bridge, word puzzles and other activities that require them to use and expand their minds. Scientific evidence increasingly points to the fact that our reasoning powers can be developed through regular exercises.

Research tells us that the television now runs about six hours per day in the average American home. TV programming in general is designed to entertain and provide an escape—not to exercise your mind. What's more, TV can be addictive. Few people who watch TV for six hours a day are even aware they invest that much time with their minds in limbo. It might be a revealing idea to log your TV time for a typical week, and contrast that with a similar log of creative activities for the same period.

7. Try not to judge too quickly.   It's true that creative people try a lot of ideas that don't work. Edison is said to have invented thousands of devices that no one has ever found a use for, and once invested more than a million dollars in a plant that never manufactured the product for which it was built. But that's not what we remember him for; we remember him for his few good ideas that changed our way of life.

Some of the best ideas in history have been discovered while someone was in hot pursuit of an unworkable idea. It's the creative process that spawns good ideas. I've found it helpful to consider *any* idea a good one, until I have spent enough time and energy on it to determine it's bad.

8. Keep your eyes open for the *winner's edge*. As a coach, I've observed that the difference between champions and losers is often incredibly slight. A gold medal track star may beat out the competition by one or two thousandths of a second. A winning horse may outdistance the field by only a nose. A star salesperson may find only one simple idea that beats the competition cold.

Living on yesterday's victories (or defeats) is a sure formula for failure. Champion marathon runners are always looking for that little something that will give them the winner's edge over the competition. They know that once they find it, it's just a matter of time before their competitors discover it and use it better, so they keep looking and reaching out.

9. Think possibilities, not problems. A century ago, a large corporation reportedly bought a huge tract of swamp land in Louisiana for a major plant they wanted to build. They sent an engineer to clear the swamp so they could begin construction. Six months later they were unable to contact him. So they sent another, more seasoned, engineer.

"PLEASE ADVISE PROGRESS CLEARING SWAMP" read the telegram they sent after not hearing from him within six months.

"NO TIME TO CLEAR SWAMP. UP TO WAIST IN ALLIGATORS" came the terse, telegraphed reply.

Finally, they sent their only available engineer— a young man with big ideas.

"SWAMP CLEARED. ALLIGATORS NOW POSE NO PROBLEM" the young man wired back three months later.

If you find you're always fighting alligators, maybe you need to put forth your best creative efforts to clear the swamp. You might even find a fortune in selling the timber or opening an alligator farm.

10. Always look for other applications of ideas. One of the greatest justifications for risking human lives and billions of dollars in space exploration is the fantastic gains from spin-offs.

Countless human lives have been saved and much suffering eliminated by the findings from space-related research and experiments. Our whole way of living and doing business has been revolutionized by spin-off discoveries in computer and communications technology, educational techniques, insulation products, nutrition and health advances and more.

Using a good idea for only one purpose is like keeping money in a sack buried in your back yard, instead of investing it for a good return.

The creative geniuses who benefit most from their ideas are not the ones who create them; they're the ones who take those ideas and apply them to a myriad of other needs and opportunities.

III. INNOVATION: CREATIVITY IN ACTION

Innovation is nothing more, nor less, than creativity in action. Nothing happens until you do something to implement an idea.

If you're a reasonably intelligent person, coming up with ideas is no challenge at all. You can dream up more good ideas than you could take advantage of in three lifetimes. The real challenge is in putting legs on your ideas.

The big difference between dreamers and innovators is that the innovators stay with an idea until they make it become a reality.

What's more, innovators make turning dreams into realities a way of life. They're always thinking and acting creatively. Sure, they fail along the way; there's always risk in trying new things. But it's that element of risk that gives life its zip. Perhaps that's why we feel sorry for dreamers, but regard innovators as heroes.

That leads us to our next chapter. How to make your dreams come true.

THINK IT THROUGH

List the three most viable ideas you've come up with during the last year, then explore what you've done with them. Consider what other benefit or use for the future the ideas might have.

	Ideas	Results	Other Benefit
1.	_____	_____	_____
	_____	_____	_____
2.	_____	_____	_____
	_____	_____	_____
3.	_____	_____	_____
	_____	_____	_____

ACTION STEP

Set aside a regular time *every day* to engage in nothing but pursuing creative ideas to make your life better. Start today!

SECTION II

THE HIGH IMPACT LIFESTYLE

CHAPTER FIVE

Goal to Go

Paul "Bear" Bryant, the legendary University of Alabama coach, was once asked by a sportscaster, "What's your secret for becoming the winningest coach in the history of college football?"

"Wellll . . . there's only two things you have to do," drawled the wily old gridiron veteran. "First, you have to keep the other team from scoring more points than you do. . . . Then you have to score more points than they do!"

That may sound like a simplistic philosophy but, as a veteran football coach myself, the Bear made a lot of sense to me. First, you have to have a good enough defense to keep from getting blown off the field. Then, you have to have an offense, and an offensive plan, which enables you to score some points of your own.

In the first section we talked a lot about how to defend yourself against the pressures of subcultures.

73

Now let's explore how to adopt an innovative lifestyle that enables you to score some points of your own.

Life's real innovators set goals and live their lives by them. Learning how to do that is precisely our goal.

I. GOALS: THE WAY YOU SHAPE YOUR OWN LIFE

"Happiness is essentially a state of going somewhere wholeheartedly," said writer W. H. Sheldon.

"For as long as I can remember," the famous Hollywood producer Samuel Goldwyn once said, "whatever I was doing at the time was the most important thing in the world for me. . . . I have found enthusiasm for work to be the most priceless ingredient in any recipe for successful living."

Perhaps those two comments explain why one leading psychiatrist recently said on national television that America could best be described as "one collective identity crisis," and another was quoted by a leading newspaper as saying the predominant condition among our citizens is "boredom."

Human beings were made to create, to achieve, to be going "somewhere wholeheartedly." Something in our mental and emotional make-up needs a challenge, an important mission to accomplish, a task that gives meaning and purpose to our existence. When we don't have it, we get bored and blue; we begin to wonder who we really are and why we're alive.

One good way to connect with this implication is to look at how many vigorous and lively people become depressed or die soon after they retire. I can't help but wonder if "Bear" Bryant's death, about a year after he set the all-time record for wins and soon retired, was not in some way related to this phenomenon.

ENTHUSIASM MAKES THE DIFFERENCE

Dr. Norman Vincent Peale makes a great point in the title of his book *Enthusiasm Makes The Difference.* Well into his eighties, he is still a vigorous and inspiring person with glorious visions for the future.

In recent years, however, the word "enthusiasm" has been so abused that it's lost all its original meaning. All the "pep talks," "motivational rallies" and empty slogans have created a feeling that enthusiasm means nothing more than "hoopla," and empty hyperbole.

But enthusiasm is a strong word, with a rich heritage. It comes from an ancient Greek word "entheos," which loosely translates "inspired by the gods." Originally, it was coined to express admiration for Olympic athletes who performed what seemed to be superhuman feats. It literally means a person who performs as if he or she "has a god inside them." Modern dictionaries define it as "a warmth of feeling, keen interest, fervor."

Let me tell you a little secret I've learned from a lifetime of coaching, guiding students and helping business leaders perform at higher levels. I can't motivate anybody! Nobody can motivate another person. Enthusiasm either grows up inside you, or it doesn't exist; it comes from the inside outward, not vice versa.

So how do you get excited about your life? How do you become inspired to achieve some overwhelming task? If it doesn't come from a powerful book, a pep talk or a rally, where does it come from?

I'm convinced that real winning enthusiasm comes from a combination of two deep inner convictions.

Enthusiasm Ingredient 1: Being Captivated by an Ideal

Real enthusiasm springs from a strong belief that something is worth doing to the best of your ability.

"Nothing great was ever accomplished without enthusiasm," said Ralph Waldo Emerson. As an anthropology major and history buff, I've observed he's right on target. The biographies of all great people reveal their deep conviction that they believed they were doing something worthwhile.

What's more, the reverse is also true. Enthusiasm does not exist in the absence of a deep conviction that a task is worthy of our best efforts. It's the belief that something is worth living and dying for that causes people to lay it all on the line, to risk everything, and to suffer untold agony without a complaint.

If you want to see your life really take off, give yourself over completely to that deepest urge within you; lose yourself in a cause you consider worthy of your very best.

Far too many people today are looking for some group, or some society, to give them something worth living and dying for. Great societies come from great people with great ideals; not vice versa.

Avoid the Escapist Mentality

When I worked as a dean in a college, I counseled many young people who told me, "I don't have the vaguest idea what I want to do with my life."

As we talked more deeply it would become apparent to me that somewhere, way down inside, there was a tiny spark of a dream that was so big it frightened them to even think about it. They found it easier to look for something else they could live with, than to risk it all shooting for the moon. Yet they could not understand why nothing else really appealed to them.

There's a part of each of us that is always looking for a place to rest, a place to feel secure, a way to escape the pains of life. It's always attractive to take the easy way out.

A major segment of our economy has grown up to satisfy this urge to be comfortable, to flee from pain, to withdraw from the battle of life. Someone, somewhere seems to have decreed that pain is not only unnecessary, but that to endure it is stupid.

The irony of the escapist mentality is that—for all its efforts to escape pain—it ultimately leads either to empty desperation or a state of constant pain.

But those hardy souls who take what Robert Frost called "The road less travelled," discover that pain is a necessary part of growth. They do not choose to suffer—to do so is a form of insanity. Rather, they choose to jump into the arena of life and give it their best shot. If that produces pain, they consider that the price they must pay for being truly alive.

Interestingly, as you read the biographies of people who've suffered greatly for their all-consuming passions, you'll notice they more often speak of their joys than of their sufferings. It's the cowardly souls, who constantly run from the tough challenges and who do most of the talking about pain.

Enthusiasm Ingredient 2: A Deep Conviction That You Can Do It

I once sat down and made a list of the twenty-two best athletes I ever coached. Then I took a look at where all their abilities took them. Only five out of the twenty-two ever used their four years of football eligibility *or* received their degrees.

What happened to the other seventeen? Most of them were actually better athletes (at least physically) than many of the players who made the teams they were trying out for. All of them had the opportunity. And, most of them were surrounded by people who believed in them.

The basic problem was that they did not believe they could accomplish what they set out to do. They started out with a burning desire to become football greats but, when the going got tough, they gave up hope.

Enthusiasm is that spark of excitement you feel when you see a tiny light at the end of a long tunnel. It's the deep inner conviction that you can win—no matter what the odds against you.

A recent Super Bowl featured two excellent teams: the Chicago Bears and the New England Patriots. Yet, only one team, the Bears, emerged the winner.

What was it that made the difference? It wasn't that one team lacked the ability: sportswriters had been talking for years about the storehouse of outstanding talent among the Patriots.

I believe you could spot the Super Bowl–winning difference in the two teams early in the season. All season long, the Patriot players and coaches had been making statements about how they hoped at least to make the play-offs. Some even confessed on television the week before the Super Bowl that they were happily surprised to be there. "I'm just glad for an opportunity to play in a Super Bowl," one of their players said a few days before the big game.

But the Bears' opening game of the season left little doubt in anybody's mind that they were a team who believed their time had come. All season they exuded a confidence that they would not only make the Super Bowl, but that they would bring home the trophy. They believed it was worth doing, and they had a deep conviction they could do it.

And so they did!

How do you develop that kind of confidence? How do you become thoroughly convinced that you can do what you most want to do in your life? Let's examine the path to High Impact Living.

II. YOU GOTTA HAVE A DREAM

If you doubt that most people have big dreams, all you need to consider is how many millions of them enter the increasingly popular sweepstakes promotions and lotteries.

I think it safe to say that anyone who reads this book would welcome a sudden windfall of several million dollars. I certainly would!

Some people hit it big that way. You occasionally read about a maintenance man or a homemaker who wins a cool $10 million in a state lottery. But for every person who wins that way, there are millions of people who never win anything. The fact is that success of any kind is seldom dumped into our lives. Sadly, in those rare cases when it does happen, it often destroys the people who are "lucky" enough to get something for nothing.

The overwhelming majority of successful people got that way by investing themselves completely in a carefully conceived plan designed to lead them to a desired destination. In other words, they had a goal, and they followed an orderly path to reach it.

In our next chapter we'll focus on how to develop a plan that will take you where you want to go in life. However, since no plan is ever any better than the goals on which it's founded, let's take a deep look at how goals can work for you. To do that, it might be helpful to think of a goal as a priceless diamond with many facets. Let's examine some of those facets.

Goal Facet 1: A Goal Is A Target

What's the first image that comes to your mind when I say the word "target"? A bull's-eye, right? It's that little dot in the center of concentric circles. It's that something you aim for and try to come as close to reaching as you possibly can.

That's precisely what a goal is. It's something you believe is worth doing, and something you feel you can do. It's something you can get excited about.

So how do you hit a bull's-eye? You close out all other images that surround you, and you focus all your attention on that tiny dot. For the moment you're fixing your aim on that target, nothing else in the world matters. The more intensely you concentrate on that target, the better your chances of hitting it.

Life goals produce exactly the same effect. They enable us to screen out everything else and concentrate all our energies and resources in a single direction.

That's a powerful reality, because concentrated energy becomes amplified power. Let me illustrate this point. If someone who weighs 120 pounds steps on your toe, it smarts a little. But let a 120-pound woman plant her spike heel there and it feels as if an elephant has crushed your toe. Engineers say that the weight, per square inch, is actually greater from a spike heel than from an elephant's foot. When you concentrate all your weight into one small area it's incredibly powerful.

A Good Goal Is Specific

All that means is that the more specific a goal, the better you chances of reaching it.

What will your life be like five years from now if you continue in your present directions, and nothing extraordinary happens to change your course?

If you're like most people, you probably have only a vague idea as to how to answer that question.

But people who build their lives around specific goals know precisely what they'll be doing five years or even ten years from now. They have a pretty good idea what their family life will be like, where they'll be in their careers, how much money they will have, and what they'll be doing socially.

Of course, no one can predict what's going to happen tomorrow or next year. But you can predict, and determine what you're going to be doing many years from now, given half the chance.

I've made an interesting observation during my years talking to people about goals. Those who live by specific goals are usually farther ahead of where they thought they'd be five years before. But those who simply take life as it comes usually say they are not nearly as far ahead as they thought they'd be five years ago. Many of them report that they are actually worse off than when they started.

The difference is that people who set specific goals make things happen. People who don't, wait for something to happen. Another way of saying it is to paraphrase the old saw: "The more specific my goals and the harder I work to meet them, the luckier I get."

Goal Facet 2: A Goal Is Achievable

A goal is not some vague pie-in-the-sky-by-and-by pipedream or some fantasy about what you wish your life could someday become. Rather, a goal is a definite target you have the resources to hit, and toward which you're working with all your might.

I've talked with a lot of salespeople who tell me, "Okay! I'm sold on setting goals! I'm going out and sell a million dollars worth of goods during the next year!" When I ask them how much they've sold during the last year, they'll say something like a tenth that much.

That's foolishness—not goal setting. Perhaps that's why so many people set goals and soon forget all about them. They set their goals so high, and place their target dates so far out into the future, that they have no hope of reaching them.

A good goal is one that causes you to stretch all your abilities, and one you're reasonably confident you can reach.

Goal Facet 3: A Goal Is a Present Reality

To really have meaning, goals must be broken down into three categories:

- Long range goals cover several years, but probably no more than ten.
- Intermediate goals are set by breaking down long range goals into annual, or semi-annual steps, always leading toward the long range goals you've set.
- Short range goals come from breaking down your intermediate goals into monthly or weekly steps toward your long range goals.

That way, everything you do tomorrow will have a definite impact on where you're going to be five years from now. It's a way of making your long range goals a present reality of your daily life.

What this does for you is enable you to concentrate all your energies on your specific goals—not just on staying busy. You'll see how important that can be when you read the chapter on time management.

A Goal Has a Timetable

Deadlines are the way you put teeth into your goals—the way you make them hold you like a vise.

For example, if you set a goal to have saved $12,000 for the down payment on a home, and you set a deadline of two years from today, you know you'll have to put aside $500 each month to reach that goal. Every month you miss will push your target date back a month.

The problem with most goals is that their timetables are so vague they can easily be fudged on. When you plan to do something in a general way (when you get around to it) it usually translates into nothing specific ever getting done.

If you want to start really getting somewhere, start setting specific goals, and giving yourself definite deadlines for reaching them—then hold yourself to them. You'll be amazed at what will happen.

Goal Facet 4: Goals Matter to You

But how do you discipline yourself to stick to the goals you set? Some people can sit down with a pocket calculator and a legal pad and come up with a plan to pay off the national debt in fifteen minutes. But nothing ever really happens.

The most frequent problem is that the goals such people set for themselves don't really matter to them, personally. They're not the kinds of targets that take over the imagination like a storm.

The key to all discipline is desire; the more you desire something, the easier self-discipline becomes. For example, it might be hard for you to boost your productivity by fifteen percent during the next year—just to prove to yourself you could do it. But if you plan to do it as a means of buying a new sports car—if that's what you really want—you'll be amazed at how much easier it will be to do.

What most modern folks do is go out and buy the sports car on credit. Then they're forced to boost their income by fifteen percent to make the payments. That's not self-discipline, it's bondage.

So, if you want to make your goals really work, choose only goals that captivate your whole mind and all your emotions. Set your sights on achieving something you can really get excited about, and self-discipline will become a snap.

Goal Facet 5: A Goal Is a Promise You Make to Yourself

Most of us are a lot better at keeping the promises we make to others than we are the promises we make to ourselves. Maybe that's why other people always seem to have more confidence in us than we have in ourselves.

One factor that causes us to be that way is that others tend to hold us to our promises, while we tend to cut ourselves a little slack—especially if we're over-committed to others.

If I promise myself a ten percent personal pay raise six months from now, I may push it back two, three or even ten months. I may never come through with it. But, if I promise that raise to someone who's working for me, I'd better come through on the precise due date or I'm in for a big morale problem.

Goals really work for us when we consider them to be promises we make to ourselves, and keep them with the same tenacity with which we'd keep a promise to our dearest loved one.

Some people even go so far as to write their goals out as a legal contract with themselves, and include penalties for default. That seems a little rigid to me, but it makes the point. At least it's helpful to set periodic review dates, when you will sit down and review your carefully written goals. Then keep that date with yourself!

Goal Facet 6: Goals Cover Every Facet of Life

Many people fail to reap the full benefit of setting goals because they confine the process to their careers. Some of the most outstanding business and civic leaders I've ever known have been complete failures in their family lives. They could tackle the greatest challenges in business and community work, and inspire hundreds of people to give their very best to help them reach their goals; but they never seemed to understand the benefit of applying the same principles to their family life.

Likewise, I've known outstanding college professors whose minds were a marvel to all around them. Yet their bodies were badly dissipated because they completely ignored their needs for physical fitness.

A good set of goals covers every area of life: career growth, family life, social development, mental/physical well-being, financial security—every part of you that you feel is important.

One way to get a handle on which areas of life really matter to you is to consider what you'd do if you suddenly discovered you only had six months to live.

You might be surprised what you'd cram into those six months. After you've thought about it a little, why not plan to get busy doing some of those things right away?

Goal Facet 7: A Goal Is a Stepping Stone

The most beautiful thing about setting and living by goals is that they keep bringing you to a place where you can set bigger and better goals. They enable you to keep expanding your horizons.

Goals also produce some fantastic side benefits. I mentioned earlier that to save $12,000 in two years, you'd need to save $500 each month. Actually, through the miracle of compounding interest and high-yield investments, you'll probably find that the last three or four months are "freebies."

Life's real winners find that at least half of the joy of having a goal is in the striving. As soon as they reach a worthwhile goal, they set another higher goal and just keep going. It's *going* somewhere wholeheartedly that produces the happiness; not just getting there.

But what happens if you don't make your goals? If you give it your best shot, you'll have the deep inner satisfaction of knowing you really tried. Like most goal setters, you'll probably double your efforts and keep at it.

What's more, you'll be miles ahead of where you'd have been otherwise. Christopher Columbus set his goal as opening a new trade route to India. He missed it by thousands of miles. But I've never heard anyone call him a failure.

III. HOW TO BECOME A PRACTICAL DREAMER

Dreams are a little like riding through a prosperous neighborhood and trying to imagine living in one of the most beautiful homes you see.

Setting goals is like picking out one of those homes, and promising yourself you'll have one just like it by a certain date.

But, if that's all that ever happens, you'll only end up frustrated. You might even come to resent the people who have the good fortune to live in those fabulous houses.

The next step involves developing a concrete plan to make it possible for you to make your dreams come true. You have to become a practical dreamer.

That's the subject of our next chapter, and the best is yet to come.

Remember: Your plan and subsequent activities will never be any better than the goals on which they are based.

THINK IT THROUGH

Write out a brief but comprehensive statement of:

A. What you think your life will be like five years from now, in each of the listed areas, if you keep doing precisely what you are now doing.

B. What you would *like* your life to be like five years from now, in each of the listed areas.

CAREER:

A. If I keep going as I am: _____

_____

B. I would like it to be: _____

_____

FAMILY:

A. If I keep going as I am: _____

_____

B. I would like it to be: _____

_____

SOCIAL LIFE:

A. If I keep going as I am: _____

_____

B. I would like it to be: _____

_____

FINANCES:

    A. If I keep going as I am: _____

    _____

    B. I would like it to be: _____

    _____

SPIRITUAL LIFE:

    A. If I keep going as I am: _____

    _____

    B. I would like it to be: _____

    _____

RECREATION:

    A. If I keep going as I am: _____

    _____

    B. I would like it to be: _____

    _____

ACTION STEP

Set aside a definite time during the next few days to formulate a complete set of goals for every area of your life. Remember to start with long range goals, then break them down into intermediate and short range goals.

Meanwhile, keep a running list of things you'd like to do during the next six months if you knew you only had six months to live. Write them down as they come to you.

Be sure to include some of those things as you formulate your goals.

CHAPTER SIX

Strategies for Success

Kemmon Williams once worked as a clerk in a popcorn stand. But this extraordinary man had a dream that would make him one of the most successful business leaders in the world.

As he tells the story, at first his dream was one day owning his own motel. From there it grew to owning a whole group of motels. Eventually, each day as he sold popcorn, he began to envision himself as "the world's greatest innkeeper."

Today, we know Kemmon Williams as the founder and long-time chief executive officer of Holiday Inns. Under his leadership that international business conglomerate and franchiser grew so that it was opening an average of one new motel room every fourteen minutes.

How did Williams go from selling popcorn to

becoming "the world's greatest innkeeper" in a few short decades?

First, he had a dream. We saw in our last chapter that success always starts with a dream, a goal, an ideal that seizes the mind and the emotions and won't let go.

Second, he had a plan. If all Kemmon Williams had done was stand behind that popcorn counter and daydream, he would have become nothing more than a clerk with big ideas—and they are a dime-a-dozen. What he did was to put legs under his dream by a carefully conceived plan that enabled him to reach his goal. Simply stated, he came up with a way to get the job done.

Third, he followed his plan to reach his goal. Making a plan was only half his battle—he had to follow that plan. He had to accomplish precisely what he had set out to do, in the way he had set out to do it.

In this chapter, I want to share with you some tested and proven techniques for turning your dreams into realities; some ways for you to go from where you are to where you want to be.

I. THE 4–10 SUCCESS FORMULA

I keep coming back to football, partially because it's a game I know and love, but also because it is such a handy metaphor for real life.

Football is a simple game. It's played by two opposing teams on a field that is 50 yards wide and 100 yards long, with a goal at each end. Each team tries to get the ball across the opponent's goal line as many times as possible during the hour the game is played, and to keep the other team from getting the ball across their own goal line.

Sounds simple enough. All you have to do is grab the ball and run 100 yards with it, right? The problem is that before you get to the goal line, you have to run through eleven big, mean guys who want desperately to stop you, and who love to bruise bodies. Very few people ever make it the entire hundred yards in one attempt.

So, to make it possible for everybody to reach the goal, the field is divided into ten-yard sections, and each team is given four tries (downs) to move the ball ten yards. If they are successful, they get four more downs.

That's precisely the way it is in real life. Few of us will ever make the big score on our first attempt at reaching a far-off goal. But we *can* put it together one step at a time.

It's what I call "The 4–10 Success Formula," and it works like this:

1. Reaching your goal is the way you score. If you get a big break and can reach your long range goal in one big attempt, obviously you take advantage of it. That seldom happens. More often, life's real winners keep their long range goals fixed clearly in their minds to help them stay on course with everything they do.

2. Your objective is to move toward your goal each day and with each action. Life has a beautiful way of rewarding achievers—it gives them bigger opportunities. When you reach one objective, that makes it possible to reach the next bigger one. Since each objective leads you in the direction of your ultimate goals, it's the way you grow.

3. Your strategies are the tactics you devise to accomplish your objectives. What matters is not simply how much you do, nor how long or often you do it. What makes the difference is what it accomplishes. The easiest or most efficient way to do something is not necessarily the most effective way to get it done.

As simple as that concept is, you'd be surprised how many people never seem to grasp it. Even if they understand it, many don't do anything with it. They're like the guy who complained to his boss that he'd had "20 years of experience," while a person who'd been promoted right past him had only five. The boss solemnly replied, "You've had one year's experience twenty times. . . . You're still doing things the same way you did when you started."

4. Your tasks are the individual steps you take to implement your strategies. The challenge is never simply to stay busy or stay around a long time. Some of the hardest-working people in the world are also some of the least successful; and they've held the same jobs for decades.

The challenge, rather, is to work hard at doing the right things and to learn how to do them in the right way. It's called "working smart."

It takes planning, perspiration, patience and persistence. But "The 4–10 Success Formula" works like nothing else.

II. PLANNING TO MAKE THINGS HAPPEN

Planning is simply choosing what you want to do (your goals); determining what it will take to get it done (your objectives), figuring out how to go about it (your strategies), and deciding on the immediate steps (tasks) you will take to start moving toward your goal.

Studies show that most people follow the path of least resistance in shaping their lives. They do what seems to be most desirable at the moment, with little thought as to where it will lead them.

When I was a college dean, I remember talking with a student who intended to quit school. He wanted to buy a car, but would have to get a job to pay for it. When I asked him why he had to have a car right then, he told me he needed it to drive to work. His game-plan was to drop out of school and get a job, so he could buy a car to drive to work. I was able to convince him that, by finishing school, he could eventually buy not just a car but the exact car he really wanted.

As faulty as that student's planning was, you'd be surprised how many people I talk with in my consulting business are living in precisely the same way. I often meet people who are leaving a job with a great future and outstanding fringe benefits, for a dead-end job that pays 25 cents per hour more with virtually no fringes.

The problem with living by impulses is that we seldom get an opportunity to make the big decisions that shape our lives. What we do is make lots of little decisions along the way, based upon what we feel at the moment. By the time a big decision comes along we've already boxed ourselves into a course of action by all the small decisions we've made. It's a way of allowing circumstances, moods and other people to dictate how we will live.

Planning lets you take a long view of all your decisions and actions. It enables you to take charge and run your own life.

Let's explore what's involved in planning with "The 4–10 Success Formula."

Planning Step 1: Goals

I hope by now you're beginning to see how important it is to have a set of specific, clearly thought out goals. It's the foundation upon which every worthwhile activity rests. Your goals are your long view of where you want to go.

Since we've talked so much about goals, and how to set them, I'll mention only one significant point here. All planning must be directed toward reaching your goals. That means you may have to pass up some good opportunities that come your way—if they lead you away from your long range goals.

That's why it's so important to set goals that truly reflect your fondest dreams and greatest hopes. It's only when you are moving steadily toward your unique place in the world that you can resist all the temptations to get sidetracked.

Planning Step 2: Objectives

Objectives make up your overall plan of action. They provide a convenient way to break down your goals into bite-sized assignments you can get your teeth into.

An objective is a concise statement of what will be required to take the first (or next) logical step in the direction of your goal.

If your long range goal is to master a certain complex subject during the next five years, a good objective would be to explore what books you will have to read, what courses you will need to take, and what will be required in time, financial resources and skills.

Most people would simply blunder into it, look to someone else to tell them what it requires, and soon become discouraged because they had not counted on the personal and financial investment required.

One benefit of planning by objectives is that often you can find shortcuts and ways to save considerable money. For example, you might discover a way of reaching your goal in four years, or even three.

The key to effective planning by objectives is to ask a lot of questions and weigh a lot of options. It requires patience, but it can save you a tremendous number of heartaches (and headaches) in the long run.

Planning Step 3: Strategies

Strategies have to do with methods and tactics. While objectives tell you what you'll need to do to reach your goal, a strategy is concerned with how you'll go about it.

To continue our example of mastering a subject in five years, some of your strategies might be:

- taking a speed reading course
- setting aside a certain number of hours each week for study
- selling something you no longer need to raise the money for the project
- looking around for good used books

Carefully developed strategies can help to save (and make) you a tremendous amount of time, energy and money. A salesperson wanting to increase total sales volume by concentrating more on larger accounts, can employ the strategy of spending eighty percent of his or her time on the accounts that produce eighty percent of sales. Studies show that most salespeople spend eighty percent of their time on the accounts that produce only twenty percent of their volume. It may take a few years to make the shift, but the increased productivity makes a lot more sense than simply sell-ing to anybody who will buy.

The same method will work in almost any field. The key is to keep asking yourself (and others) how you can increase your effectiveness at everything you do.

Planning Step 4: Tasks

Tasks are the individual steps you take to lead you to your goals. Taking carefully planned steps leads you in the direction of your goals. Merely staying busy eats up all your time, resources and energies without really moving you ahead.

Planners concentrate on their goals; activists con-centrate on their activities. Activists say at the end of a day, "Boy! I'm tired! I sure worked hard today!" But planners say, "Wow! I really made progress today!"

Let's stick with our example of mastering a sub-ject. A planned step might be to learn what is needed to enable you to pass an upcoming test. Instead of saying, "I studied three hours last night," you would say, "Now I'm ready for that test." It might sound like a small distinction, but the end result can be enormous.

Think for a moment about how the strategic task approach can be applied to almost any situation. Instead of saying, "I spent four hours doing paperwork," you might find yourself saying, "I found a way to do all my paperwork in two hours." Instead of saying, "I called on ten clients today," you might say, "I closed more sales in less time today."

There's an old myth in American culture that says those who work the hardest are the ones who get rich. I've discovered very often the opposite is true. People who are into hard work tend to see themselves as working for money. People who are into planning tend to think of how their money can work for them.

One reason the Japanese have beaten us out of so many markets in recent years is the difference in the way workers in Japan view their income and the way it's viewed by most Americans. In this country, we talk about the income we have left after we've paid all our taxes and bills as "disposable income"—money that is ours to spend as we choose. In Japan, they talk about "retained income."

The same principle applies to our work habits. We talk about how much we're making per hour. They focus on how much they're getting done.

If you want to see a marked increase in your living standard, learn to plan your work carefully so every task you do will lead you closer to your goals. Remember, you're always working for yourself—no matter who signs your check. The better you become at what you do, the more valuable you will become to whoever you call boss.

III. WORK YOUR PLAN

It's vital to have a good plan for everything you set out to do, but even the best-laid plan won't work unless you do.

Now I would guess you're a pretty energetic soul who is willing to invest time and energy in becoming more productive, or you wouldn't have read this far. So this is not going to be a pep talk on the value of hard work.

Rather, I want to highlight the biggest flaw in most planning. It is simply that people don't follow through on the plans they've so carefully laid. As important as a well designed plan is, it is only a statement of what could be. Remember the poet's words, " . . . of all sad words of tongue or pen, the saddest are these: 'It might have been!' "

People who really make their plans work for them not only stick tenaciously to those plans, they do it in an organized way. Just as they've thought through what they're going to do and how they will do it, they think through how they will keep tabs on how well they're doing. They use follow-up techniques.

Follow-up Technique 1: Get Yourself Organized

Most people waste vast amounts of time doing things in a disorganized way. The time you spend wading through clutter, looking for things you've misplaced, correcting mistakes, and following outdated systems or procedures is time you could be investing in reaching your goals.

This is such a vital subject, we will explore it much more fully in the chapter on time management. For now, let me simply point out that organizing is a crucial part of planning, and an extremely important part of following up on your plans.

Follow-up Technique 2: Monitor Your Progress

Always think results, and constantly test to see that you're getting the results you want.

Effective managers of other people know that just because a task is assigned, does not necessarily mean it gets done. They check to make sure it's done, and done correctly. Yet many managers (and most people) often fail to monitor their own progress.

One of the most effective tools for monitoring your progress is to keep a "to do" list. No., I'm not suggesting you merely write down everything you can think of that you need to get done during a given day. What I'm suggesting is a strategic planning "to do" list.

Here's how you do it. You consult your plan at the end of each day, and choose the most important things on that plan. Write down all of them you think you can reasonably get done. Next, you rate them according to their priority level. The most important task becomes your number one priority for the next day. The second most important, your number two priority, and so on.

When you start out the next day, start with your number one priority and concentrate on it until you either get it done or decide it can better be done later. When you've finished with number one, move on to number two.

It's a convenient way of making sure you stay busy doing the right things, and it gives you a simple tool for measuring your progress every day.

Follow-up Technique 3: Check Your Schedules

Always include in your plans some regularly scheduled checkpoints at which you review your overall progress toward reaching your goals. It's important to realize that each missed deadline not only pushes the realization of your goals back by that much time, it can sabotage your whole plan.

Many successful leaders use a system called CPM–PERT, which stands for Critical Path Method— Project Evaluation and Review Technique. It's a complex name but a simple idea that basically means that every task along the way impacts on every other task. If one task is not done by its scheduled time, it delays all other related tasks.

What it can do for personal planning is to help you evaluate, in advance, what certain actions will do to your overall plan. For example, by looking at your whole picture, you can see how taking an afternoon off will impact on what you need to get done during the rest of a week. It might reveal that taking Monday afternoon off to play a round of golf will cause you to miss an appointment which will push back other things you need to get done that week. However, you might discover that you could take off Thursday afternoon without causing any delays.

Regardless of how you do it, the important thing is to keep tabs on your schedule so that you are always on course toward your goals and the deadlines you have set.

Follow-up Technique 4: Hurry Up Every Chance You Get

This technique involves basically three things.

First, it means learning to distinguish between what's important and what is urgent. Always giving in to the urgent is called the fireman approach—you're always running around putting out fires. Answering the phone may seem urgent at the moment, but if it disrupts your whole schedule by interrupting you in the middle of an important task, it might be more productive to call the person back later. The best way to tell what's important from what only seems urgent is to keep asking yourself what each bid for your attention will mean six months from now.

Second, it means constantly learning how to do things better, and in less time. The time you use looking for a better way can be some of the most valuable time you invest. Simple things such as carefully reading instruction booklets for new equipment and talking to experts can often show you how to use the equipment to gain shortcuts in other applications. For example, I once talked with a guy who had used a personal computer for two years before he found out he could use the data he'd stored to do his income taxes each year.

Third, it means avoiding the temptation to waste precious time, when you discover you're ahead of schedule. If you're oriented toward staying busy, a break in your workload means only one thing—take the time to goof off. It's the same principle that causes a person to say, "Hey! I just paid off my car, so I can buy a boat." Goal-oriented people say, "Hey! That means I've got a few extra bucks to invest so I can get rich enough to buy all the boats I want."

Now, I like to goof off about as much as anybody I know. That's why I build plenty of leisure time into my hectic schedule. But the time I gain by learning how to do things quicker, can usually be better invested in stepping up the schedules that are taking me to my goals.

TYING IT ALL TOGETHER

Kemmon Williams (remember, he's the popcorn clerk who became "the world's greatest innkeeper") had a dream. But he would have remained a clerk for life if he had not developed a systematic strategy for putting legs on his dream. He became a master planner by using the tips and techniques we've covered in this chapter.

THINK IT THROUGH

Use the form below to develop (or review) your own goals, objectives and strategies for each of the listed areas. Also, list the first task you must complete for each. If you have difficulty with this exercise, I would suggest you re-read this chapter. It's extremely important!

CAREER:

Goals: _____

_____

_____

Objectives: _____

_____

_____

Strategies: _____

_____

_____

First Task: _____

FAMILY:

Goals: _____

_____

_____

Objectives: _____

_____

_____

Strategies: _____

_____

_____

First Task: _____

SOCIAL LIFE:

Goals: _____

_____

_____

Objectives: _____

_____

_____

Strategies: _____

_____

_____

First Task: _____

FINANCES:

Goals: _____

_____

_____

Objectives: _____

_____

_____

Strategies: _____

_____

_____

First Task: _____

ACTION STEP

Set aside a definite time when you will take out a day or two to develop your own plan. Then do it! I promise, you'll be further ahead a year from now than you will by just staying busy during that time.

Don't Let Time Hold You Hostage

No one needs to tell you how important it is to use your time wisely. You already know that, or you wouldn't be reading a chapter on time management. So I won't waste your time by trying to make you feel guilty about letting time slip away.

Instead, I'll give you some practical ideas that have worked well for me and thousands of other people. I hope you'll find some insights you can use to gain better control of your time rather than allowing it to hold you hostage.

Understanding Time Management

"Time is the scarcest resource," according to management expert Peter Drucker, "Unless it is managed nothing else can be managed."

Technically, as I'm sure the professor would agree, we can't manage time at all because we have no control over it. This "Paradox of Time," by Henry Austin Dobson, expresses it very poignantly:

"Time goes, you say? Ah no!
Alas, Time stays, we go."

All we can really do is to manage our uses of time. So, when we speak of time management, we are actually talking about self-management.

Self-management in time utilization involves keeping tabs on six factors, which I call the six "p's": purpose, patterns, plans, parasites, performance and persistence. Let's see how you can make better use of time by watching your "p's".

I. THE POWER OF PURPOSE

The most pressing question about activities is not "What are you doing?" but "Why are you doing it?"

You can work hard all day every day, and still not get much done. The question is not "how hard do you work?" but "what do you work at doing?" "Busy work" is not productive because it doesn't go anywhere—no matter how much time and energy it eats up.

Focus on goals, not on activities. Any time you feel yourself rushing like mad and still coming up short on time, review your day to see if what you've been working on is leading you toward your goals.

Wasting motion is wasting time, and wasting time is wasting your life.

Most of us manage our money down to the last penny. We know precisely how much we have coming in, and exactly where it's going. We draw up budgets and discipline ourselves to live by them. If we don't, we'll soon find ourselves broke and head-over-heels in debt.

Unfortunately, far too many people fail to apply the same principles of management to their time—though it is much more valuable than money.

Protect Your Prime Time

The major television networks diligently guard the hours from eight to eleven each night. They know that's when they will have their largest audiences and, thus, when they can make the most money by selling commercials. They call it "prime time."

All of us have certain hours of each day that offer us greater opportunities and challenges than any other time during that day. It may be because we are more alert and productive during those hours, or because other people are most cooperative with us then.

Whatever the reason, learn to identify your prime time and guard it with a passion. Use it only for working toward your goals, for doing the most creative tasks, and for accomplishing what's most important. You can do the urgent things at other times.

II. PINPOINTING PATTERNS

The first step in managing your time is knowing precisely where it goes. Sure, most of us can have a general idea where our time goes. We know we work so many hours each day, we sleep so many hours, we spend some time eating, and so forth.

But how do we spend our time working? Or playing? Or doing anything else? The fact is that most of us simply don't know.

Let me suggest a very effective tactic for analyzing your time habits.

Keep a Time Log

There's only one sure way to find out where all your time goes: keep a detailed time log for a definite period and carefully analyze what you do with your time.

Now, before you say, "I don't have time to mess with that," and brush the idea aside, let me tell you some of the fantastic benefits of keeping a time log.

1. You'll discover some gaps you can plug up and save yourself a bunch of time.
2. You'll probably find there are certain times of the day, and certain days of the week you tend to waste more time than others. That will give you a basis for improving your scheduling.
3. You will probably discover that you are more productive at certain times of the day. You can schedule important tasks during your peak performance periods.
4. When you realize how much time you spend on certain activities, you might feel it is all out of proportion to their significance. You can start looking for ways to cut the time you devote to them.
5. You might also discover some very important activities that are being slighted, and you can plan to give them the time they deserve.
6. You'll only have to do it periodically for it to be very helpful to you. Once you see where your time goes you can make the rational decisions necessary to assure that you manage your time rather than allowing it to manage you.

7. Perhaps the most important of all, it's the only way you can really know for sure where you spend your time. Until you keep a detailed time log, you can only guess where your time goes.

The mechanics of keeping a time log are quite simple. All you do is write down what you do during each quarter hour or so of whatever time you're logging. Be careful not to change your regular routines so you'll get an accurate picture.

After you've kept a detailed log for two weeks or so, look it over very carefully. Analyze specifically which activities get the most amounts of time and rate them as to priority. Search for time-wasting actions and loopholes. Study the amount of time you spend with certain people and decide if it's justified. Pinpoint as precisely as you can the hours of the day when you are most productive, and those times you are least productive.

You can use the time log to study everything about the way you spend your time. Believe me, if you'll take it seriously, two weeks of keeping a time log will completely change the way you relate to using your time.

III. A PLAGUE OF PARASITES

There's a big difference in donating blood and being drained by a parasite. When you donate blood, you do it willingly and gain the personal satisfaction of knowing you might have saved someone's life. But a parasite attaches itself to you, without permission, and steals your very life.

Time-wasting habits can rob you of your most vital possession—your very own life—and give little or nothing in return. Consider these research findings:

- The average worker wastes 40 percent of a typical day.
- The average manager is interrupted every three to nine minutes, and it takes him or her twice as long to get back on track.
- At best, only two of every ten people can be considered good time managers.

It sounds as if there are a lot of parasites on the loose in most workplaces. If you really want to gain control of your time, you simply must find and root out the time-wasters. You might even find it helpful to think of them as burglars who steal your most prized possessions—the irreplaceable moments of your life.

Stage Your Own Burglar Hunt

Here's an excellent tactic for discovering the activities that most frequently waste your time. Keep a running list of all time-wasting activities you notice during the next week. Each time you find yourself engaged in a time-waster, write down the amount of time you waste. Then add up the total times of each of your biggest time wasters. You might find it very revealing.

To get you started, here is a list of the most common ways people waste time. It is from *Get The Best From Yourself*, by Nido R. Qubein, and reflects research data from many sources.

1. Procrastination—putting things off until they end up requiring more time or until they gang up on you and take control of your schedule.
2. Trying to complete tasks for which you don't have enough information.
3. Doing unnecessary routine work—just because you've always done it.
4. Unnecessary distractions or interruptions.

5. Sloppy use of the telephone.
6. Unnecessary meetings, or meetings that last too long.
7. Failure to delegate tasks to capable people.
8. Lack of self-discipline in matters of time.
9. Failure to set priorities.
10. Unnecessary shuffling of mail and paperwork.
11. Excessive socializing.
12. Lack of mental control or concentration—daydreaming at the wrong times.
13. Lack of knowledge about your job.
14. Stretching your refreshment breaks.
15. Refusing to say no to things that interfere with your priorities.
16. Making careless mistakes that necessitate redoing work.
17. Sloppy or ineffective communications.
18. Failure to use management aids (like dictating machines, message centers, etc.) to full advantage.
19. Bulky, poorly designed systems or procedures.
20. Failure to insist that your co-workers carry their part of the load.

You might be able to add several to the list, and maybe you don't waste time in all the most common ways listed above. The important thing is that you identify the ways in which you do waste time.

Once you have the culprits in your sights, don't let them get away. One by one eliminate them, until they are all gone.

IV. PRODUCTIVE PLANS

If you aim at nothing, you'll hit it every time.
The key to all effective time management is plan-

ning. That word scares many people, but it need not scare you. Planning merely means "a systematic strategy of applied consistency." In simpler terms: plan your life and live your plan.

Here are some planning pointers, all of which are based on the section on planning in chapter five.

Planning Pointer 1:
Make Planning A Way Of Life

Planning your time is deciding in advance what you're going to do and how you're going to do it, allocating the time needed to get it done, and following the plan you have laid. It can be as complex as a CPM-PERT program on a massive computer, or as simple as a few notes scribbled on a napkin. The important thing is that you do it and that you apply it to every area of your life.

Planning Pointer 2:
Put Yourself On A Schedule

Most people, given the choice, would say they'd rather live without a schedule. Unfortunately, there is no such thing as unscheduled living. You either decide your own schedule, or let other people or circumstances decide it for you.

In reality, a schedule is nothing to be feared, it's simply a roadmap to guide you through the day. Of course the more complete it is, the more it can help you save time. For example, instead of merely setting aside certain hours for work, why not allocate definite time periods to accomplish specific tasks?

Planning Pointer 3:
Get Your Whole Life Organized

The least productive people in the world are not necessarily lazy; they're just disorganized. In fact, some of the hardest working people in the world work much more than they need to because they are so disorganized.

Disorganized people usually work frantically all day, conscientiously try to get everything done, and leave work tense because of important reports unfinished, major tasks uncompleted, and people still waiting to see them.

Getting organized can help you work more easily, get more done, and make you more valuable to any organization. It keeps you from reinventing the wheel every time you need a ride, wasting energy and time on lost motion and feeling frustrated because you can't find things.

Here are some ideas that can help you get organized and stay that way.

1. Don't just shuffle papers—process them. Picking up the same piece of paper again and again is a waste of time. If it's important enough to act upon, act. If it's not important enough for a decision, either file it or throw it away.

2. Keep your life uncluttered. I love the philosophy of Andy Rooney, of *60 Minutes.* He says he has a rule that for everything new that comes in the front door, something of equal size has to go out the back door. It's not a bad idea.

Excessive clutter complicates every task, wastes valuable time and leads to mistakes. You'll be amazed at how much your productivity will improve, and how much more you'll enjoy your whole life, if you'll simply designate a place for everything and keep everything in its designated place.

3. Practice decisiveness. One thing that keeps people from being organized is that they hate to make decisions. The better you become at making decisions, the more promotable you become. Don't flounder around all day, sorting through more and more facts. Gather a reasonable amount of information, study it and make a decision.

Certainly, you'll make mistakes. The only way to keep from making mistakes is to do nothing, and that's the biggest mistake of all. Besides, studies show that decisive people actually make fewer mistakes than people who struggle endlessly over every choice they must make.

Planning Pointer 4: Keep Your Priorities Straight With "To Do" Lists

In chapter five we pointed out that the "to do" list is one of the most effective devices for sticking to your goals. It's also a great technique for managing your time. It is also one of the simplest tools to use.

All you do is take a few minutes at the end of each day to write down the five to ten *most important* things you need to get done the next day. Then arrange them numerically by priorities. The next morning, start with your number one priority and move through the list until you've accomplished them all. As simple as it is, it can do wonders to save you time and help you avoid frustration.

"This is the most practical lesson I've ever learned," Charles Schwab, founder of Bethlehem Steel, told a group of young executives. "I had put off making a phone call for nine months," he explained, "so I decided to list it as my number one task on the next day's agenda. That call netted us $2 million because of a new order for steel beams." From that moment on, Mr. Schwab became an avid fan of "to do" lists—and he didn't do badly for himself.

Living by "to do" lists is the best way to ensure that you concentrate on what's really important and not on things that only seem urgent at the moment.

V. PEAK PERFORMANCE

I've always thought of myself as a hard worker. In fact, I used to put in 14 or 15-hour days and was constantly rushing around trying to get everything done. I lived under unrelenting stress, and had developed numerous stress-related problems, including colitis.

In 1979 I attended a time management seminar and discovered *why* I was having to work so hard for so long every day. My problem was that, while I was working very hard, I was not working very smart.

Peak Performance Principle 1: Peak Performance Means Concentrating on Results—Not Activities

As a coach I had always chosen my starting line-up on the basis of one overriding principle: I wanted the twenty-two players who would consistently give me their peak performances when it counted most—during the games.

All I had to do was to apply that same principle

to my own life and work. I needed to be at my best, at those times that called for my best performance.

That's when I discovered the simple, but profound, Pareto Principle, which implies that 80 percent of one's results come from 20 percent of one's activities. It's the famous 80/20 rule of time management.

What if, I began to reason, I could consciously devote 80 percent of my time to the accomplishment of those activities that accounted for 80 percent of my results? The implications were astounding! That would mean I could achieve peak effectiveness 80 percent of the time.

So that's precisely what I started trying to achieve, and it has made me much more productive *and* given me much more spare time. Think for a moment about what that could mean in your own situation.

What makes it all possible is getting and keeping your priorities straight. You have to think **results!** That means you have to learn how to weed out all the nonproductive activities that eat up so much valuable time, and focus all your efforts on doing the most productive task, at the most productive time, and in the most productive way.

Try it! It really works!

Peak Performance Principle 2: Learn to Delegate

One way always to be sure you are investing your efforts in the most productive ways is to learn how to delegate.

Before you jump to the conclusion that this section has no meaning for you, if you have no employees, let me assure you that it applies even more to those who have no one working "under" them.

Let me illustrate. If you were being paid $10 per hour, it wouldn't make much sense to take two days off to do a repair on your own car that a mechanic would charge $50 to do for you, would it? The net cost of that do-it-yourself repair job would be $130—plus parts.

All you need to do is to apply that principle to all the possibilities of your prime time, and you will begin to see how effective delegation can enable you to spend your time where it will get you the biggest results.

There are several keys to effective delegation.

First, learn what to delegate. The best way to do that is to evaluate each task you face on the basis of this simple question: Is this the most productive way to use my time? Another very helpful question is: What's the most productive use of my time right now?

If a proposed task is not the most productive use of your time, start looking around for some way to get it done for you—even if it costs you some money.

Second, learn how to delegate. The biggest reason people fail to do exactly what delegators want done is that they don't understand what is expected of them, or how to do it. When you assign a task, make sure the person understands fully what you want and when you want it, and that they have all the information and resources they need to get it done.

Third, learn what and to whom to delegate. All of us have certain abilities, interests and resources that enable us to do certain things better than anyone else. Search out the most qualified person to do each task.

Delegation also includes learning to use the myriad of time-saving devices available. You might be amazed at how much of your prime time can be saved by a better use of dictating and answering machines, personal computers and word processors, paging services, etc.

Fourth, quit being a perfectionist. Ego is the greatest single reason most people won't delegate even their most routine tasks. Face the fact that no one will do anything exactly as you would do it. Then ask yourself if it is essential to your goals that each task be done the way you'd do it. If the answer is yes, ask if the task is worthy of your best efforts. If not, delegate it or forget it.

You might be in for a happy surprise with many tasks. People who start delegating for the first time, often discover that others can actually do them better, and in less time. It's rough on the ego, but that is softened by the increase in your effectiveness.

Peak Performance Principle 3: Develop Time Awareness

Most of us have little concept about how much time it takes to do any given task. We almost always underestimate. Thus, we tend not to allocate enough time to many tasks we do, then we feel frustrated because we can't accomplish it all.

Murphy is right, you know, "Anything that can go wrong will go wrong." And he's also right in one of his corollaries, "Everything takes more time than we expect."

Conversely, we tend to let many precious moments in each hour slip away because we simply don't pay attention to where they go.

To combat this, each time you find yourself wasting time, imagine an alarm going off inside, and charge yourself an imaginary fine of a dollar. Total it up at the end of the day and learn how much it's cost you. To see how much your time is worth, consult the chart below and find the salary you'd like to be making:

Time Value Chart

ANNUAL INCOME	EACH HOUR IS WORTH	EACH MINUTE IS WORTH	AN HOUR A DAY FOR A YEAR IS WORTH
$10,000	$ 5.16	$.0864	$1259
12,000	6.16	.1024	1503
14,000	7.16	.1192	1748
16,000	8.16	.1360	1992
20,000	10.32	.1728	2518
25,000	12.81	.2134	3125
30,000	15.37	.2561	3750
35,000	17.93	.2988	4375
40,000	20.64	.3596	5036
50,000	25.62	.4268	6250

The table is based on 244 working days of 8 hours each. By saving one hour each working day during a normal career, you can add the equivalent of six years of productivity. That's better than retiring early, with full benefits.

Make no mistake about it—the more productive you become, the more valuable you are to your employer.

The impact is equally dramatic in your personal life. For example, if you lie in bed fifteen minutes after your alarm goes off, spend fifteen minutes trying to find something to wear (because you didn't select your clothes last night), wait fifteen minutes for your spouse to get out of the bathroom, and spend another fifteen minutes rushing to the store because you're out of milk, you've wasted an hour you could have spent having fun.

It takes a little effort to become time conscious, but it pays rich dividends.

VI. PURSUING PERSISTENCE

Finally, what do you do when you have to wait for someone, even when you have an appointment? Or you get stuck in a traffic jam? Or take a long ride on an airliner?

It's easy to sit and stew away precious minutes or even hours. That's letting circumstances and people run your life.

Learn To Use Little Bits Of Time

You'll find you can rescue that lost time by keeping handy some worthwhile tasks to do. For example, it's a good time to catch up on your reading, not the outdated and irrelevant magazines usually available in waiting rooms. Or, you can use that time to do some of your routine paperwork.

By being creative about it, you can process some of your best ideas or write down new ones. While stranded in a traffic jam, Noel Coward took out a pen and paper and wrote "I'll See You Again."

Don't let the time-wasters steal your life. Use your imagination to come up with productive uses for time you spent waiting for someone or something beyond your control. It will not only save you time, it'll help you keep stress under control.

Manage Interruptions

Many people find themselves managed by interruptions. A co-worker drops in for a friendly chat, you get a dozen phone calls, or you spend an hour looking for something. But interruptions can mangle your life—especially if they occur during your prime times.

Here are a few suggestions for managing interruptions:

1. Control your telephone time by only taking calls during certain hours, being direct and to the point, collecting all the information you need and listing what you want to cover, before you make a call, and hanging up as soon as you finish your business.

2. Manage "live" interruptions by going to the other person's office whenever possible, removing extra chairs from your office, having an understanding with co-workers that you're not to be disturbed during certain time periods, standing up when someone enters your office and remaining on your feet until they leave.

3. Avoid having to look for things during peak periods by assembling everything you need before you begin working on a project.

Remember—you either manage interruptions or they will mangle your time.

Enjoy Your Free Time

Face the fact that you owe it to yourself, to your loved ones and even to your bosses to get plenty of rest and recreation. It's the only way you can be your best.

Nowhere is self-discipline more important than in the matter of taking time to recharge your batteries. Our bodies, minds and psyches are structured so that they must have time to renew themselves. Otherwise, you will always be operating below your capacity.

One of the all-time great success motivators, Dale Carnegie, often used a story to illustrate this point. Two woodcutters were hired to clear a large tract of land. One worked at breakneck speed all day. The other stopped every hour or so to take a break. At the end of the first day, the frantic worker noticed that the other fellow's pile of wood was much larger than his.

"I don't understand!" he complained. "My axe has struck every time yours has today. Besides, I've worked straight through, while you sat down for about five minutes out of every hour. . . . Yet you've cut more wood than I have!"

"Did you notice," said the wise old wood cutter, "that while I was sitting, I was sharpening my axe?"

That's what relaxing is all about—it's sharpening your axe so that you can work more effectively.

TYING IT ALL TOGETHER

There's only one way to keep time from holding you hostage—you have to watch the six "p's" we've discussed in this chapter.

Just as it's important to apply goal-setting to every area of your life, it's equally important to apply time-management techniques to all areas. I like the way it's expressed in the following lines:

Allow time for work; it's the price of success.
Allow time for love; it's the sacrament of life.
Allow time to play; it's the secret of youth.
Allow time to read; it's the foundation of knowledge.

Lost time does not return. You will never have more time than you have now, but if you use it wisely it's all the time you need.

In the spirit of that reminder, why not allow some time to look more closely at ways of making better use of your own time? The following exercise can help you do just that.

THINK IT THROUGH

Make a list of the most common ways you waste time each week, a method for overcoming each, and an estimate of the time you could save by eliminating the wasteful practice. At the end, add up the time you could save during a typical week. Then figure (based on your weekly income level) how much money you could save by plugging up the gaps.

Time Waster	Time Saver	Time Saved
_____	_____	_____
_____	_____	_____
_____	_____	_____
_____	_____	_____
_____	_____	_____
_____	_____	_____
_____	_____	_____
_____	_____	_____
_____	_____	_____
_____	_____	_____
_____	_____	_____
_____	_____	_____

Total time to be saved weekly: _____

Net value of time saved: _____

ACTION STEP

Start immediately keeping a time log, and analyze your time habits for the next two weeks. Then develop strategies to get better control of your time usage. It'll save you loads of time in the weeks and years to come.

CHAPTER EIGHT

Do It Now . . . Always!

Do you ever find yourself saying things like, "Someday, I'll really get myself organized," or "I'll go on a diet . . . but not 'til next Monday," or "I should get involved in that project soon, but. . ."?

Procrastination is a real trap for most people— even those who are otherwise high achievers. In fact, many of the brightest, most energetic people in business are held back by the habit of constantly putting things off.

The sad fact is, that all too often, people clutter up their environments with useless relics of the past, and clutter up their minds with important things to be done . . . someday.

Now, That's Procrastination!

The story is told of a guy who was clearing out a long-unused desk stored in his garage and came across an old shoe repair claim check.

Just for fun he stuck it into his pocket and stopped by the shoe repair shop, thinking surely the shoes had long since been thrown away. He was curious to see what the cobbler would do.

To his surprise the old shoemaker took the claim check, squinted at it, and disappeared into the back room of the cluttered little shop. Several minutes later, he emerged and handed the check back to the man, and matter of factly said, "They'll be ready next Thursday."

Now, that's what I call procrastination.

Let's explore two big questions: Why do people procrastinate? How can you overcome the problem?

I. WHY PEOPLE PROCRASTINATE

Procrastination is a problem.

People can never reach a significant portion of their potential until they develop the habit of doing *it now.*

Virtually every time management expert I know of advocates do-it-now behavior as a necessary ingredient of time management.

Studies show that most people agree they should not put things off, and yet they still do it.

So, if everybody recognizes procrastination as a problem, and nobody wants to do it, why do so many of us do it so often?

Perhaps as you read through this list of the most common reasons people procrastinate you can get a handle on the key reasons you so often fall into the procrastination trap. Later we'll explore some solutions to this nagging problem that holds so many people back from reaching their full potential.

Procrastination Reason 1

We con ourselves into thinking there will be a more convenient time later, or that the task will be easier to do at another place or time. This is what happens with most large, or unpleasant tasks.

The truth is that a project that is put off usually gets put off again and again, and so keeps getting bigger or more unpleasant.

Why is there never enough time to do it when it first comes up, but always time to do it when it finally catches up with us?

Procrastination Reason 2

We're not sufficiently motivated by the importance of a task to do it promptly. Projects that are long-range, that have been delegated to us by someone else, or that we find dull often get put aside in favor of more interesting work. Unfortunately, the dullest drudgery can lead to the most exciting results.

Procrastination Reason 3

We may procrastinate because we're not pressed for completion. We're not given an immediate deadline, so we put the job off. It's tough for many people to be self-starting and self-disciplined. They respond only to pressure imposed by someone else—even though they often resent that pressure.

Procrastination Reason 4

Our work environment is so out of control that we simply can't find the time to do an assigned task. We allow a continuous flow of distractions, disturbances and interruptions to prevent us from doing any meaningful work. In this kind of environment, it's easy to keep putting an important task aside—sometimes never to return to it.

Procrastination Reason 5

Excessive clutter and disorganization in our work environment can often be pegged as the culprit. We have so much junk lying around that it's hard to find a place to work, or we are so disorganized it's hard to get anything done.

Procrastination Reason 6

We may procrastinate because we are faced with a task that is so unpleasant that we can't bring ourselves to do it: firing someone we like, dealing with an irate customer or giving someone bad news.

Unfortunately, even though we put off doing them, we don't get them off our minds. The longer we wait, the worse we feel about what must be done. If we let these unpleasant jobs pile up sufficiently, we can become a bundle of nerves.

Procrastination Reason 7

By far the most common reason is that procrastination becomes a way of life for us. We do it with our work, so that we have to stay late or bring it home with us. We do it in our private lives, so that we're always having to break into our work schedules for personal reasons. We do it in our social lives and end up wishing we could get out of engagements we made months ago with great expectations.

Procrastinating means we are constantly in a got-to-catch-up mode that keeps us frustrated, depressed, less productive and more stressed.

Procrastination can cause tremendous mental and physical strain, can consume our creative energy and rob us of our zest.

II. BREAKING THE PROCRASTINATION HABIT

Kicking the procrastination habit might be one of the toughest challenges you'll ever face, but it can be one of the most rewarding investments you'll ever make.

Here are some tested and proven techniques for breaking free of the debilitating and career-stifling habit of putting things off.

Procrastination Habit Breaker 1: Focus On The Benefits

If your procrastination habit is long-standing, chances are it's deeply imbedded in your subconscious mind. When you hear "Do it now!" your subconscious wants to know "What's in it for me?" Focus on some of the many benefits you'll receive from breaking the nasty procrastination habit. Here are a few of the more outstanding benefits most people enjoy when they kick the habit.

1. Less stress—You will find yourself working in a more relaxed manner, enjoying it more and feeling much less pressure. Your energy level will go up markedly.

2. More quality free time—Procrastination is a tremendous time-waster that robs you of time you could spend doing things you really enjoy. As you become more efficient and effective, you'll have increased leisure time and be able to enjoy it more fully.

3. More enjoyment—Your enjoyment of everything you do will be enhanced once you remove the drudgery of carrying the extra weight of a myriad of unfinished tasks.

4. Higher self-esteem—You'll like yourself better, and feel more self-respect when you start getting most things done on time.

5. It will get easier—As hard as it may be to believe, it won't always be difficult to avoid putting things off. You'll actually come to enjoy it within a very short time.

6. More money—That's right! The less you procrastinate over important matters, the more promotable you'll become.

Those are only a sampling of the common benefits people experience when they kick the habit. You will undoubtedly be able to add several personal benefits to this list. The important thing is to keep reminding yourself of what's in it for you.

Procrastination Habit Breaker 2: Get Organized, Starting Now

The easiest way to break a bad habit is to start a new, good habit. Start out small and work your way into it gradually. Begin with one small task, in one area of your life. When you've completed it, move on to a bigger one. Keep expanding your new habit of being organized into every area of your life.

Procrastination Habit Breaker 3: Set Up Some Victories For Yourself

Create an inventory of tasks and projects that have been hanging around for a long time. Then set up a realistic schedule—one you know you can live with—for getting them done. Adopt that as one of your top priorities, and stick with it. As you complete each task or project, stage a mini-celebration of your victory and reward yourself.

Make a mental game out of it. One executive I know hates to return phone calls and has always put them off until they piled up. So he has conquered the problem by scheduling the period just before lunch as his time for returning calls. He rewards himself by spending fifty cents on his lunch for each call he returns. To get dessert, he has to be pretty effective. That tactic has the added benefit of providing a strong incentive for keeping his calls brief.

Procrastination Habit Breaker 4: Tackle Unpleasant Tasks Early Each Day

"Kiss a frog first thing every morning, and nothing worse will happen to you all day." I wouldn't go that far, but that is a humorous way of expressing a real truth: If you've got something unpleasant to do, do it and get it out of the way. The later in the day you schedule an unpleasant task, the easier it will be to put it off and the longer you'll have it weighing on your mind.

Procrastination Habit Breaker 5:
Change Your Attitudes

Adopt a positive mental attitude about your work. Remind yourself that everybody has work that they are less than thrilled about doing. Abraham Lincoln said, "Most people are about as happy as they make up their minds to be." That bit of wisdom can easily be paraphrased to read, "Most people enjoy their work about as much as they make up their minds to."

Learn how to see unpleasant tasks as opportunities to grow, to develop patience and self-discipline, and to become more effective with other people. Rid your vocabulary of words like "chore."

Procrastination Habit Breaker 6:
Use Visual Reminders

Many outstanding business leaders post signs around in their offices, cars, and near all their phones, to serve as constant reminders. The signs say things like, "Do it now!" and "What's the best possible use of my time right now?" and "Time is money!"

A doctor I know who hates filling out the forms he has to send to insurance companies for payment for his services has instructed his assistant to staple a photocopy of a $100 bill to each form he must fill out. This visual reminder that each completed form brings in money helps him to dig in more quickly.

Additionally, it's a good idea to avoid using any negative reminders, such as signs like "Bless this mess," or "The hurrier I go, the behinder I get!" They send a signal to your subconscious mind to accept procrastination, clutter and disorganization as normal.

Procrastination Habit Breaker 7: Be Decisive About Projects You Accept

Before you take on a new project, look for a place in your schedule for it. If you don't have a definite time available, turn it down. If it's from your boss, tell him or her what you've got scheduled, and ask if the new task should take precedence over work already assigned.

Remember that everything takes longer than you expect, and allow some extra time for all new projects.

One of the most common traps is scheduling projects a long time in advance. If you give some people enough lead time, they'll agree to do anything, even if they really don't want to do it. Somehow, they kid themselves into thinking the deadline will never come, the job will just go away, or that their tastes will change. Remember that every new project you take on limits your options for accepting or rejecting other future projects.

Procrastination Habit Breaker 8: Practice, Practice, Practice

Habits are formed by repetition. A habit is merely an action you've taken so many times it becomes automatic—you can do it without having to think about it. That's why it's so easy to procrastinate.

Apply that same principle to developing the positive habit of doing things as they come up. Keep practicing until it becomes an automatic response to any project that comes your way.

TYING IT ALL TOGETHER

Procrastination is a thief that robs you of energy, time, self-respect, motivation, advancement, money—even life itself.

Surveys show that more than half of all Americans vehemently dislike their jobs and careers. Statistics also show that more than 95 percent of all the people reaching retirement age have achieved little financial success and end up dependent upon Social Security, other government programs and relatives.

How can someone get caught in the trap of getting up every morning to go to a job they hate? How can rational people reach retirement age with nothing set aside?

All too often, the answer is procrastination. "As soon as the kids are grown," or "As soon as I get a little ahead," or "Someday . . ." they keep saying to themselves. And, before you know it, it's all over.

Procrastination is more than an annoying little fetish. It's a destructive habit that robs you of your greatest opportunities and robs the world of your greatest ideas and talents.

It's vital that you take action on it now!

THINK IT THROUGH

Maybe you don't realize how much you actually procrastinate. Most people have no idea how often they put things off. Before you put it off again, try to get a handle on how much and why you procrastinate.

Make a list of all the tasks and projects you now have to do (in every area of your life), and determine how many of them are running behind. What percentage of your work—and even your pleasure—is now being delayed?

ACTION STEP

Pick one area of your life in which you tend to procrastinate and start today clearing out all the clutter and every unfinished task. Believe me, you'll like yourself, and your life, a lot better.

CHAPTER NINE

Mastering Communication Skills for Success

The single most important ingredient for success in any career, relationship or interpersonal activity is effective communication.

Oh, I know in business, and often in our personal lives, we say things like: "I don't want talk. I want action!" and "Cut through the fat and tell me the bottom line!" and "It's not what you say, but what you do that counts!"

However, the most frequently traveled road to action, to the bottom line, and to getting people to do what we want them to do is effective communication.

The Key Word Is *Effective*

Effective communication is one of the most vital activities of human beings. Yet it's one of the most hazardous of all human endeavors, and it's becoming a bigger challenge every day.

The problem is not that we don't talk to each other anymore—we talk too much, if anything. Everywhere you turn, someone is trying to tell someone else something.

The problem is that we don't communicate **effectively**. We send messages others don't receive, or receive incorrectly. We don't pick up the meanings of messages others send to us. We ignore the power of nonverbal messages, both going out and coming in.

"Speech is a joint game between the talker and the listener against the forces of confusion. Unless both make the effort, interpersonal communication is quite hopeless," said communications expert Norbert Weiner.

The Four Skills Of Effective Communicating

Effective communications come as a result of mastering four basic skills:

1. Managing time
2. Receiving and understanding messages
3. Sending effective verbal messages
4. Sending and receiving nonverbal messages.

You can only become an effective communicator when you master each of these four skills. Being unskilled in any one of them will keep you from getting the results you want.

The purpose of this chapter is to enable you to get a clearer understanding of how each of the dimensions can work for or against you, and to offer suggestions as to how you can improve your batting average as a communicator.

I. MANAGING TIME

After many years of conducting seminars and consulting with business leaders about how to become more successful through better time management, I'm convinced that both the greatest cause and most frequent result of poor communication is poor time management.

That statement may surprise you, since most people don't associate time management with communicating. But, as we go along, you'll see that effective communication has everything to do with time management.

First, let's look at how poor communication results in poor time utilization.

The High Cost of Poor Communication

Many people have little concept of how poor communicating creates time-consuming problems, increases their workload and wastes many golden opportunities.

How many times have you found yourself saying things like: "That's not what I told you I wanted!" or "How many times do I have to tell you. . . !" or "But, you said. . . !" If you're like most people, chances are pretty good you say such things fairly frequently.

The specialists in the communications field say that at least 80 percent of all business-related problems can be traced to poor communications. On a personal level, most marriage counselors agree that upwards of 90 percent of all marital problems stem from difficulties in communicating.

Let's be very practical about it. It doesn't take an accountant to figure out that all the money wasted in

American business in one year on needless mistakes, lost or poorly used time and materials, and the loss of customers and valued employees would more than pay off the national debt. And we have the nerve to talk about government waste!

By far, the greatest contributing factor to poor time utilization is ineffective communications.

Pinpointing The Cause Of Poor Communications

Did you ever stop to think that the greatest reason for poor communications is poor time management?

Again and again, after I've sorted through all the data my clients bring to me about their inefficiency and poor productivity, the root of the problem can be traced to one of two things:

1. Somebody doesn't take the time to send the right message
2. Somebody doesn't take the time to receive the right message.

More often than not, both problems are present. In any case, the root cause of the problem is poor time management; people simply are **not taking the time** to communicate **effectively**.

The 80/20 Rule— With A Twist

Ask most business executives (and anybody who works with people) where they spend the bulk of their time, and they'll tell you quickly—solving problems! Press them further and they'll admit that what the communications specialists say is true—most of their problems come from faulty communication.

We have already talked about the ineffectiveness of spending 80 percent of your time on activities that produce 20 percent of your results.

What if we could free up half of the time we spend solving problems, doing or getting things done over or wondering what to do? I believe we can do at least that well by better managing the time we put into communicating—sending and receiving messages.

How can we do that? How can we become better communicators by becoming better time managers? The obvious answer is by putting more time into communicating.

Yet, for most of us, the obvious answer is neither feasible nor correct. We're geared for speed; the whole business environment is geared for speed. Besides, most of us already spend too much time talking and listening.

It's Not What You Do, But The Way You Do It

Let's go back to one of the basics of time management—the most **efficient** way to do things is not necessarily the most **effective** way to do them.

The question is not, "How much time do you spend communicating?" but, "How do you spend that time?"

Learning how to communicate more effectively is quite likely the greatest single time management investment tip I could pass along to you at this point. In the remainder of this chapter, we'll learn some tested and proven techniques—tactics used by many of the top professional communicators in this country. So let me suggest you invest considerable time reading and re-reading these pointers.

II. MANAGE YOUR RECEIVING AND UNDERSTANDING MESSAGES

Receiving and understanding messages is a crucial area of communicating effectively. The odd thing is that most of our attention focuses on the sending of messages.

Legendary pianist Arthur Rubinstein, who had mastered eight languages, once told an amusing story on himself.

He developed a severe and stubborn case of hoarseness, some years ago, and as a smoker he feared the worst. He consulted a leading throat specialist.

"I searched his face for the slightest clue during the thirty-minute examination," said Rubinstein, "but he was expressionless. He told me to come back the next day. I went home full of fears, and I didn't sleep that night."

The next day he went through another long and silent examination.

"Tell me," the grand old maestro shouted. "I can stand the truth. I've lived a full, rich life. What's wrong with me?"

After a long pause, the physician gave his expert diagnosis: "You talk too much."

All Effective Communication Is Dialogue

"Every man is a potential adversary, even those whom we love," wrote Reuel L. Howe, in *The Miracle of Dialogue*. "Only through dialogue are we saved from this enmity toward one another."

Professor Howe defines dialogue as getting "into significant touch with someone."

The reason all effective communication is dialogue is that it involves more than words. It has to do with meanings, feelings and understandings. Only human beings have the capacity to grasp each other's meanings, to care about each other's feelings and concerns and to understand each other. As remarkable as they are, you can't communicate with a computer.

It is only when we connect fully with others that we begin the process of conveying our meanings, our feelings and, in a sense, ourselves.

Mastering The Art Of Paying Attention

No real communication can take place until somebody pays attention.

We want others to pay attention to us. Yet there are so many voices screaming for attention it seems ours gets lost in the shuffle. Amusing radio and television commercials cry for attention, newspapers and magazines use clever graphics and slogans, people at home make bids for attention, co-workers and bosses try to get attention, and so on.

In this age of exploding knowledge and noisy information, it's not surprising that more and more people are paying less and less attention. Keeping up with the input from so many sources is enough to short-circuit even the most brilliant minds.

How can you break through all that interference and make sure that people elect to pay attention to you? **The best way to get others to pay attention to you is to pay attention to them.**

We humans want to be understood, to matter to others, to know that others concern themselves with what matters to us. In short, we want others to pay attention to us, and when they do, we reciprocate by paying attention to them.

It all boils down to this: **the key to all effective communication is identification.** People pay attention to what matters to them. If you want to get a grandfather's attention, talk to him about his grandchild . . . instant attention! If you want a golfer's attention, talk to him or her about golf . . . rapt attention!

When you show interest in what matters to a person, you can expect that person to listen to what matters to you.

"I don't have time for all that junk!" you protest. "Keep it simple and get right to the bottom line. . . . I don't want to get that involved with people."

I'm not suggesting that you waste a lot of time on small talk. What I'm advocating is that you really pay attention to what the person is saying about the subject at hand.

The High Cost Of Not Paying Attention To Others

How much time do you lose by not paying attention to others?

1. It costs you time because you don't understand what they say, or, perhaps what they mean. Maybe you've been in one of those seemingly endless meetings in which the two sides were close to an agreement, but kept talking for hours because each refused to pay attention to what the other was saying. It's as if they were talking in different languages.

"Why didn't you say that in the first place!" someone finally shouts.

"I did say that! You just didn't listen!" comes the retort. Then they're off again on an endless debate over who said what. All that confusion can be eliminated if we will just pay attention to each other.

2. You lose time because you make more mistakes. The waiter who half-hears an order, the executive who half-hears a complaint or idea, the parent who half-hears a child's request all could save themselves and others a lot of time and grief by taking time to pay attention.

3. You lose time because you have to repeat yourself, and people still don't get your messages. If you treat co-workers like robots, don't be surprised if they pay little attention to your requests, or even your orders. Identify with their concerns and you'll be amazed at how seldom you have to repeat your requests.

4. Failing to pay attention to others costs you time because you fail to discover their misconceptions about you or what you're saying. It's often a simple matter to correct a mistaken notion someone has about you; but first you have to know that they have the misconception.

5. When you're too busy, or too preoccupied to pay attention to others, it can cost you time. You can easily miss valuable information that could help you accomplish your goals. For example, a salesperson may be so busy trying to sell a benefit the account considers insignificant that he or she misses a comment about another benefit that could instantly close the sale. The seller may make the sale eventually, but could have saved a lot of valuable time by paying attention.

I don't want to belabor the point with other examples; your attention might begin to wander. But you understand, don't you? If you'll pay attention to others it will save you time and they will help you get what you want by paying attention to you.

That brings us to the question of how to pay attention to others. I have three suggestions:

1. Actively Listen

Studies show that most people think of themselves as good listeners. Yet the same research continuously confirms that the average person seldom really listens to others.

Did you notice I said *listen* not *hear?* Hearing is the physical response of the ears. Listening, however, is the active process of deciphering signals and translating them into meanings. It's the precise opposite of talking. When you talk, you are concerned with what goes out. When you listen, you are concerned with what comes in.

Most people are much more adept at expressing their feelings and concerns than they are at listening to the feelings and concerns of others. It's the reason we have so much "monolog in duet." When you say what you thought up while the other person is saying what he or she thought up while you were talking.

Poor communicators monopolize the talking, effective communicators monopolize the listening.

Tips On Active Listening

Here are some tested and proven tips to help you become a good listener:

1. Open your mind and ears. Switch off all negative thoughts and feelings about the person and be receptive to the messages he or she is giving.

2. Listen from the first sentence. Put aside what you're doing or preoccupied with and give your undivided attention. If you can't do that at the moment, suggest a time when you can.

3. Analyze what is being said. Even the slowest listeners can think faster than the fastest talkers. Avoid trying to figure out what the person is going to say—you may miss what he or she actually says. Instead, use your faster thinking speed to analyze what is *being* said.

4. Really listen, don't just *not talk*. Active listening is not only a great communication skill, it's also an important human relations skill. Always assist the other person in conveying his or her meanings accurately to you.

5. Never interrupt, but always be interruptible! Nothing cuts off the flow of meaningful dialogue quite as effectively as continuous interruptions. What's more, it's offensive and rude.

6. Ask questions. To stimulate people to talk and to help you clarify your understanding of what they mean, let them know you take them seriously by drawing them out.

7. Remember what is said. Log important points into your mental computer. Take notes if necessary. Look for connections between apparently isolated remarks.

8. Block out interruptions and distractions. Concentrate so fully on what's being said that you don't even notice visual and audible distractions.

9. Be responsive. Get your whole body into listening and showing that you are paying attention. Look the person squarely in the eyes, use facial expressions and gestures to show you hear and understand what's being said.

10. Stay cool! Don't overreact to highly charged words and tones. Hear the person out, then respond. You'll be amazed at how often people cool down and begin to talk calmly, once they have vented their anger or frustration.

Remember, your goal is to be an effective communicator, not to merely "get in your two cents worth."

Believe me, as an educator, coach, professional speaker and business executive for many years, I've noticed that the people who are most effective at getting across their points to others, and getting things done, are those who do the best job of listening to others.

2. Be A Good Observer

More than 65 percent of what we learn we learn through our eyes, according to research psychologists. Studies also show that some people are more observant than others, and thus learn faster and more completely.

Just as there's a difference between *hearing* and *listening,* there's also a big difference in *seeing* and *observing.* Seeing is a physical response of our eyes to lightwaves as they fall upon patterns, textures and shapes. But observing is an active pursuit that involves the conscious mind. It's seeking to record data into the memory, to assimilate that data into intelligible signals, and to translate it into meanings.

The better you become at observing, the better you can become as a communicator. Everything you observe, while receiving and sending messages, is potentially useful.

It starts with your perspective. Since what we observe is influenced by what we feel, think and desire, each of us observes things differently. Good observers try to put aside their biases and prejudices and observe as objectively as they can.

Your vantage point can also influence what you observe. That's why three people who see the same accident will often describe it totally differently. Effective communicators seek to see things from several vantage points before they jump to conclusions.

I'll have much more to say about nonverbal communications, later in this chapter. For now, suffice it to say that the more observant you become, the more effective you will be as a communicator.

3. Seek To Understand

Signals always have meanings behind them. They almost never come to us as passive or meaningless information.

For example, if someone yells, "Fire!" we immediately start trying to find out what that means to us. We want to know where it is, what danger it poses to us, and how we can escape that danger if it's present.

One thing that makes communicating so hazardous is that words often have so many different meanings. "Fire" can mean a consuming heat, to let a person go or to excite enthusiasm. Fire is what you do when you shoot a gun, when you put ceramics into a kiln or when you start up your car. You could probably come up with many more uses for that one little word.

The 500 most commonly used words in the English language have more than 14,000 different meanings. What's more, the same words have different meanings to different people, and in different contexts.

Effective communicators learn to wade through all that confusion to seek for the meanings behind the words and actions of others. They constantly keep their eyes and their minds open so they can observe anything that might help them grasp the meaning of what is being said. And they frequently use the six great detectives of understanding: who, what, when, where, why and how.

Avoiding The Two Big Barriers of Understanding

Without doubt, the greatest barrier to understanding is haste. We simply don't take time to assimilate and comprehend the meaning of what's being said or done.

The rush to understand is what causes most of our mistakes and the mistakes of others. It triggers confusion and conflict that will have to be dealt with later, and it shuts off some of our greatest opportunities.

It's simple to break through the haste barrier, but it's seldom easy. All you have to do is slow down and make sure you understand what's happening all the time.

The second great barrier of understanding is what I call the "top this" syndrome. When someone tells us a story, we've always got to try to top it with a story of our own. When someone expresses a problem or a concern, we've got to tell why ours is greater. When someone wants to make a point, we always seem to think ours is more important.

An effective communicator works hard to combat this enemy by being receptive to other people. When others genuinely believe we take them seriously, they will become much more open about the meanings behind their words.

To Pull It All Together . . .

"God gave us two eyes and two ears, but only one mouth; so he must have meant for us to observe and listen twice as much as we talk." That bit of down-home wisdom makes a lot of sense, even in this scientific age with all its sophisticated communications devices. It also explains why I've devoted more than half this chapter on communication to the receiving end.

Modern technology enables us to send and receive more and faster messages, but until we become robots we will focus most of our attention on meanings, feelings, desires and concerns. I vote for staying human.

It is only when we master the skill of effective listening that we can begin to master the other two.

III. MANAGE YOUR MESSAGE SENDING

Poor communicators say, "I tell it like it is and don't care what people think about it!" Most people resist them.

Mediocre communicators say, "All I can do is tell it like it is and it's their responsibility to hear it!" Most people ignore or misunderstand them.

Effective communicators say, "I make sure they know what I mean!" Most people understand them, and many give the response they desire.

If you want "the bottom line," I'll give it to you up front: **the central purpose of all communication is to gain a desired response.** When you talk, you want action. You want people to laugh or cry with you, to care about what matters to you, to understand how you feel and what you want, and often you want them to do something.

Before any of that can happen, they have to receive and understand your meanings. Only then can they respond.

Effective communicators assume full responsibility for making sure others receive and understand their messages.

I've developed seven strategies for reducing communications misfires. Let me give them to you straight:

Strategy 1:
Be Definitive

Say what you mean. Say precisely what you mean. Say only what you mean.

The English language is a confusing compendium of words with multiple meanings. We connect these words into phrases that often are vague, ambiguous and open to many interpretations. Then we use these imprecise phrases as verbal shorthand. Is it any wonder that everybody's confused?

Think about these commonly used phrases and instructions:

- "Give me a call later and we'll discuss it." Later that morning? That day? That week? When? What exactly does "later" mean?
- "That could cost a lot of money!" What exactly is "a lot of money"? Is the statement intended to stop the person from pursuing the project? Simply to encourage caution? What does it mean?

Work at saying exactly what you mean, with words and phrases that are clear enough to be understood. Avoid saying things that are open to interpretation.

Strategy 2:
Don't Make Assumptions

When you assume you "take for granted." You base your communication on what a person *ought* to know or understand, rather than on what you clearly communicate to them. But there is often a vast difference in what ought to be known, and what is actually known.

Making assumptions is asking for trouble. They are shortcuts that usually come back to haunt you. They can create problems that are far more time-consuming than clear communication at the start would have been.

It is actually more efficient to over-instruct, than to under-instruct.

Strategy 3:
Avoid Unfamiliar Language

Jargon, technical terms or slang words may be quite clear to you, but they can be a foreign language to others. To complicate the problem, people are often embarrassed to tell you they don't know what you're talking about, or they may think they understand when they really don't.

Every sphere of human activity provides ample opportunity for this communication misfire. Salespeople, for example, often drift into using technical terms that are common to their associates, but extremely confusing to their clients.

Listen for, list and actively avoid any terms that are clear to you but might be confusing to others. If you know what you're talking about, you don't need to impress anybody with technical jargon. If you don't know what you're talking about, no amount of jargon will impress anyone.

Strategy 4:
Be Aware Of Losing Your Audience

Remember, effective communication can only take place when two or more people are paying attention to each other. The instant attention is lost, effective communication stops. This is true whether you're speaking in front of a crowd or one-to-one.

The attention span of the typical person in our society seems to be shrinking. Maybe it's because people watch so much television, with its scene changes every few seconds. Perhaps it's because the pace of life is accelerating so rapidly that people have more to think about today. For whatever reasons, all of us have to fight for each other's attention more today than ever before.

Learn to say things concisely. Practice presenting your ideas in a structured way that is easy to follow. Get your thoughts organized before you start talking. Be animated when you talk. Make it as easy as possible for people to pay attention to you.

But, even when you are doing all that, face the fact that people—for their own reasons—will drift away while you are talking with them. When that happens, do something to get their attention, or stop wasting your time trying to communicate with them.

Strategy 5:
Get Feedback

Your goal is to have your messages received, understood and acted upon. Smart communicators constantly test to make sure that is happening with each interchange. They constantly ask for feedback. They seek to discover what their audiences have understood them to say.

The quality of the feedback you get will usually be determined by the types of questions you ask. Closed-ended questions that require a yes or no response, don't help much. If you ask, "Do you understand?" people will usually say they understand rather than risk embarrassment, to appease you or as a way to cut short the conversation.

I urge you use open-ended questions such as, "How do you think that applies to your staff?" or "What do you think would be the impact of that decision?" They force people to give you clues as to how much they understand.

Be careful, however, not to create the impression that you are grilling the person to see if they are listening. Make sure they understand that you are testing the communications process, not threatening or condescending to them.

Strategy 6:
Give Feedback

Whether you are receiving a message or testing a message you've sent, always give voluntary feedback. That way, the other person will know you understand what they're saying to you.

Never hesitate to ask for clarification. It's better to be sure than to be wrong later.

Strategy 7:
Give Effective Communication A High Priority

If you want to invest your energies and resources in an activity that will pay big dividends in time saved, problems avoided and opportunities seized, make effective communication one of your highest priorities. The pay-off will be fantastic!

1. Try to communicate under the right conditions. Don't hold important conversations while you're rushing down the hall to your next meeting.
2. Take copious notes. Don't depend on your memory.
3. Confirm important conversations with a letter or memo. It can greatly reduce misunderstandings.
4. Understand that communicating is a hazardous pursuit and do all you can to reduce the risks of misfires.
5. Take the time to learn all you can about how to do it well. Read everything you can get your hands on about the art of communicating, listen to cassettes by experts and attend seminars as often as possible. It's a great investment.

IV. MANAGING YOUR NONVERBAL MESSAGES

Educators say we learn as much as 70 percent of what we know through our eyes. That means the vast majority of what we communicate to others is through nonverbal signals—clothing, gestures, body language and even eye movements.

A salesperson with the greatest product in the world, in front of just the right prospect, can lose an almost certain sale because of the way he or she looks. A member of the opposite sex can completely misunderstand the motivation behind a reassuring touch.

A complex negotiation can break down at the most critical moment because someone carelessly makes the wrong gesture.

Nonverbal communication is far too important a subject to be covered adequately as a sub-section in a chapter. All I can do is tell you how important it is and point out some crucial areas to watch. You'll find some excellent books on the subject in the business or communications sections of any good library or bookstore.

People *Hear* The Way You Look

The way you look sets the stage for whatever you say. In the critical first two or three minutes after meeting a stranger, we make up our minds as to how receptive we will be to anything he or she does or says.

Of course it's a free country, and you can look any way you choose. But it is also true that people have the right to tune you in or out.

If you want to be heard, always look your best. You never get a second chance to make a first impression.

People *Hear* The Way You Act

Good communicators are also good actors. They know that people watch their facial expressions, their body language, their gestures and everything they do.

Actually, what you do often has a great impact on the way people interpret what you say. For example, if you smile broadly, make a feeble gesture toward a door, and say "Let's go!" somebody might rise to follow you. But if you pull off your coat, ball up your fists, put on a snarling expression and then say "Let's go!" you'd better be ready for action.

Sure, that's an extreme example, but those little

gestures, facial expressions and body movements play a bigger role in communicating than many of us realize.

TYING IT ALL TOGETHER

Effective communication is both an art and a science.

As an art, it can always be improved, it lends itself to personal adaptations and it can be a great source of enrichment for every area of your life. As a science, it has certain guidelines and ground rules that must be followed.

The more you study and practice it, the better you can become. And the better you communicate the more you can get what you want out of life.

THINK IT THROUGH

Explore how you can apply to your life what's been said in this chapter about each of the four communications skills:

1. Managing time to communicate effectively

_____

_____

2. Receiving and understanding messages

_____

_____

3. Sending effective verbal messages

_____

_____

4. Sending and receiving nonverbal messages.

_____

_____

ACTION STEP

Set three objectives for improving your communications skills:

1. _____.

2. _____.

3. _____.

SECTION III

High Impact
Adapting

CHAPTER TEN

Managing Stress

Adaptive people experience as much stress as anyone—sometimes even more. But it doesn't seem to bother them as much as it does the people who have not learned to roll with life's punches.

Whatever your goals, your chances of reaching them will be proportional to how well you manage stress. Make no mistake about it—stress can and must be managed. The ability to manage stress is one of the most vital skills for success, no matter how you define success.

In this chapter, we're going to explore what stress can do to you and what causes it. But mostly we'll seek to discover how adaptive living can enable you to manage stress in your life, and even use it to help increase your impact.

"STRESS!" You've probably seen that sign in offices printed in fuzzy letters that blur. It's a word that's cropping up more and more these days.

The dictionary defines stress as "Strain . . . from pressure."

Maybe that's the way you feel a lot of the time, strained by all the pressure in your life. If so, this chapter could be one of real value to you. We're going to explore what stress can do to you, and where it comes from. But mostly we'll seek to discover what you can do to overcome it.

I. WHAT CAN STRESS DO TO YOU?

Too much stress can:

- Wreck your health by causing indigestion, heart disease, high blood pressure, headaches, etc.
- Wreck your emotions by causing depression, anxiety and even some forms of mental illness.
- Wreck your performance by reducing both its quantity and quality, and by making your work erratic.
- Wreck your relationships by making you irritable, perpetually tired and even chemically dependent.

Enough stress can even kill you!

But, it's not all bad news! Some stress, handled correctly, can actually be good for you. But let's hold that one, while we try to get a handle on exactly what stress is.

What Is Stress?

According to Hans Selye, M.D., one of the world's foremost authorities on stress, it is "the non-specific response of the body to any demand."

Dr. Selye uses words like strain, pressure and intensity to describe the conditions surrounding stress.

Most authorities agree that each of us experiences stress differently. It can cause one athlete to be alert and give a peak performance, yet cause another to fall apart at the most critical moment. It often drives one executive to brilliant and creative achievements, yet forces another into severe physical problems and early retirement or death.

II. WHAT CAUSES STRESS?

Where does all that pressure, strain and intensity come from?

"My job!" is the most common answer. Others high on the list include: "My spouse!" "Financial pressure!" "Too much change!"

The reason I ended all those responses with an exclamation point is that's the way most people answer my question—with an exclamation.

What all those people are describing is tension, not stress. Tension is the combination of external forces that tug at us. And, heaven knows there are plenty of them! Most of us are constantly caught in a tug-of-war between one subculture and another, stretched tightly by career pressures, tossed about by change— it's enough to make you tense!

Stress is our *reaction* to all that pressure. It's the way your body, mind and emotions respond to tension.

I've Got Good News!

The fact is that whatever level of stress you feel is *your own creation*. It is not the pressure in your life that causes your stress—it's your reaction to that pressure.

This is not an accusation. It's the greatest discovery you can make about stress. When you can truly say to yourself, "I cause my own stress!" you can quit trying to fix the blame and start fixing the problem.

Do you realize how great that news is? It means that you are not a helpless victim of external pressures beyond your control. If you cause your own stress, you can do something about it.

I've Got Even Better News!

Some stress is actually good for you! It can add zest to your routine, joy to your relationships, years to your life.

Let's look at a few of the latest findings of experts in the field of stress management:

1. Stress can contribute to your health by aiding your digestion and relaxation, improving your cardiovascular system and relieving other physical problems.
2. Stress can aid your mental/emotional health by providing stimulation and even exhilaration.
3. Stress can improve your performance by making you more alert, more stable and more productive.
4. Stress can improve your relationships with

others by making them more interesting and challenging.

5. Stress can prolong your life by giving you a constant challenge.

Stress is that excitement you feel when you know the stakes are high, but you are so exhilarated you don't want to quit. It's that sense of anticipation you experience when you believe something exciting is about to happen. It's sometimes that signal that lets you know it's time for you to make a change.

What makes the difference as to whether your stress becomes *distress* or puts *zing* in your life is how you control it. It's that simple!

But remember, what is simple is not always easy!

May I Tell You My Favorite Golf Story?

If all this talk about stress is making you feel uptight, let me tell you my favorite golf story. Don't stop me if you've heard it, because it's got a point.

After fifteen years of watching Joe go to play golf every Saturday morning, his wife talked him into letting her go along to see what he found so compelling about the game. After all, it was the only thing Joe ever did so faithfully.

On the way, he explained the game to her. "You hit this little ball with this club," he demonstrated, "and knock it into the little hole in the ground."

When they reached the course, Joe teed off, watched the ball soar right down the fairway, bounce a couple of times when it hit the green and rolled right into the cup—a HOLE-IN-ONE!

Joe went bonkers! It was his first ace—ever! And, at least six people had seen it! He started jumping up and down, throwing clubs in the air and yelling to the top of his lungs.

"I've never seen you like this!" his wife shouted.

"I got the ball in the hole in one stroke!" he tried to explain.

"So what? Wasn't that what was supposed to happen?" she asked.

So what does that have to do with controlling stress? A great deal! Let me explain.

Your system is designed to operate at its peak, when you have just the right amount of stress and are handling it correctly. Your mind, emotions and body form a perfect synergy when they are in harmony. That's what's "supposed to happen."

As I'm sure you know, it's not that easy.

I don't propose to make it easy, but I *will* try to keep it simple, as we explore how to control stress.

III. HOW CAN YOU CONTROL STRESS

Stress has always been a fact of life, and with all the sweeping and accelerating changes we face today, it is a bigger factor than ever.

But you don't have to face it all alone. Much research has been done and published in the area of stress management in recent decades.

Another thing going for you is that most of the findings agree on certain basic factors about stress and ways of dealing with the problems it can create. Let's look at several of those highly productive keys to understanding and managing stress.

KEYS TO TAKING CHARGE OF STRESS

1. Learn To Recognize Stress And Its Impact On You

We are all individuals, with differing personalities, emotions, bodies and values, so stress affects each of us differently. Here are some common symptoms that can be your tip off that stress is causing problems for you:

- Excessive weight gain or loss
- Loss of appetite or compulsive eating
- Frequent heartburn
- Chronic diarrhea or constipation
- Insomnia
- Frequent headaches
- Constant fatigue
- A frequent need for medicines
- Dependency on drugs or chemicals
- Muscle spasms
- Shortness of breath
- An inability to cry or a tendency to burst into tears easily
- Persistent sexual problems
- Depression, anxiety, irritability or other emotional problems

All of these are easily detectable, but may not be caused by stress. If a problem persists, you should see your doctor right away. There are other symptoms of stress that doctors use special tests and procedures to determine. So your doctor may tell you that you have stress-related problems that do not appear on this list.

When there is any question, follow your doctor's advice or get a second opinion.

The important thing is that you learn to recognize when you are suffering from too much stress.

2. Decide To Take Control Of Stress

Decide to do it. It's that simple. Stop "chasing your own tail" long enough to objectively evaluate your situation, your problems, your opportunities and, most important of all, your options.

There's no point in spending your time thinking about what others could do about it, or what others are doing to contribute to it. You cannot control what others do. And you can't look to others to solve the problem.

But you can control what you do. You can control the way you think, your attitudes, your schedule and the people with whom you spend time.

If stress is creating distress for you, it's virtually impossible to conquer it all at once. You can't just wave a magic wand and make it disappear. But making that initial decision to conquer it is the first big step toward recovery.

Get control of your life, one day at a time—starting today.

3. Rediscover Hope

Re-kindle the flame of hope within you. Get in touch with your most meaningful and inspiring goals—those dreams for making tomorrow a better day.

Most of the leading authorities on stress management agree that people who have little or no hope usually make no progress toward controlling stress.

It's when hope springs up inside that a new direction can begin.

4. Get Serious About Time Management

In a way, stress is like alcoholism or drug addiction. At first, it's only a symptom of a deeper problem, but eventually, it becomes the problem. Just as an alcoholic needs to stay away from booze, you need to do something to reduce the stress-generating pressure you're under. Absolutely nothing holds the promise of reducing the pressure as effectively as good time management.

I first became involved in time management in 1979, and it literally may have saved my life. When I learned how to quit putting in the 14- and 15-hour days just to stay even, the changes in my mental and physical health, lifestyle and business were sweeping and almost instantaneous.

If you're having a real problem with stress, let me urge you to go back and re-read the chapter on time management and start taking a committed approach to getting control of your schedule. It's a great way to regain control of your life.

5. Learn To Use Stress Control Techniques

There are many very effective techniques to help you gain and keep control of stress in your life. Here are a few suggestions:

1. Work off stress through regular and vigorous exercise such as walking, jogging, running, swimming, tennis, golf, gardening, etc.

Note: If you are over forty, or have not been exercising it's a good idea to have a medical checkup before you start any program of physical exertion.

2. Talk out your anxieties and worries with someone you respect and trust. It can be a friend, a family member, a minister, a counselor, a teacher or anyone who will lend a willing ear. If you are seriously anxious much of the time, see a professional counselor.

3. Face up to unpleasant facts and get it over with. There may be some circumstances you just can't do anything about. Don't let needless worry take over and ruin your life. Accept them for what they are, and make the best of them. You might even be able to turn them into blessings if you work at it creatively enough.

Also, if you've got an unpleasant decision to make or a bad job to do, don't put it off. The longer you wait, the worse the stress it will cause. As soon as you have enough information or resources to act, bite the bullet and get on with it. You'll often be amazed at how small some huge decisions will look after they are made.

4. Stay away from self-medication. Drugs, including alcohol, that only hide stress from you don't help anything, and *can* make it a lot worse in the long run. If you need help in getting off alcohol or drugs, don't put it off—get help now.

5. Get as much sleep as you need. Everyone's body needs a different amount of rest. Too much or too little sleep can make you feel drowsy and could damage your health. Check to see what amount of sleep works best for you, then stick to getting that amount every night.

Also, it's a good idea not to eat too heavily at night, especially near bedtime. Too much or the wrong types of foods can do terrible things to your sleep.

If stress persistently keeps you awake at night, see your doctor.

6. Allow some time to goof off.   All work and no play invites stress to take over your life. A pleasant hobby, a social calendar and some good old-fashioned goofing off can do wonders to relieve stress.

7 Cultivate strong relationships.   Take time to enjoy your family and friends and build supportive relationships. You'll find them a constant source of release from stress.

There are many other stress arresters available. These are only a few of the obvious ones. You're a unique individual. Use your creativity to find what works best for you. The important thing is that you arrest stress before it causes distress for you and others you love.

8. Watch what you eat and drink.   Most experts now agree that good nutrition can do wonders for curing excessive stress. One of the newest cures is also one of the oldest preventions, "you become what you eat."

9. Look into various relaxation therapies.   Many people have found a great deal of help in biofeedback techniques, meditation and even hypnosis. Explore those areas to see if they offer something for you. Be careful about "quack remedies" being sold for big bucks. Consult your doctor, if you have questions.

10. Cultivate a sense of humor.   The Bible is on target when it calls laughter "the best medicine." Don't take everything that happens so seriously. Learn to see the humor in life. Read some books just for fun. Go see a funny show. Do some frivolous things along the way. It'll do wonders for your stress level.

6. Build Your Own Life

"Don't do what you sincerely don't want to do. Never confuse movement with action," said Ernest Hemingway. That's great advice for combatting stress.

Here is a series of principles that I developed as a result of suffering from the anguish of a stress-related illness during the first years of my college coaching career. They have certainly helped me over the years and I offer them to you as signposts on the road to decreasing stress in your life.

- Compete against the achievement of your objectives, not against the successes of others or their expectations of you.
- Strive to be the best you that you can. It's all you ever can be anyway.
- Don't try to be "all things to all people." You'll end up being nothing to anybody, especially yourself.
- Be sure to engage in conflict only over things of significant consequence to your long term goals.
- Maintain a positive belief system and set of expectations. At the very least, remain neutral and become positive as your expectations are fulfilled.
- Avoid procrastination like the plague.
- Dwell on your past successes. View past failures only as lessons learned.
- Life is a continuous series of opportunities. The way we handle opportunity is the way we handle our lives.
- There are no rules of success that will work unless you do. The secret, however, is not only

to work hard, but, more important, to work smart.
■ Associate with positive, successful people and you will be more positive and successful.

These are the guidelines of a perspective on life. Living within these guidelines will do wonders to relieve a life plagued by the agony of stress!

7. Choose Your Own Perspective

Robert Louis Stevenson lived before the age of antibiotics and was constantly plagued by consumption and often bedridden for months at a time. But the disease never crushed his enthusiasm for life.

His wife heard him coughing badly one day and said, "I expect you still believe it's a wonderful day."

"I do," he replied. Then sitting up in the bed, he asked her to remove a row of medicine bottles from his windowsill.

"Why should I do that?" the discouraged woman asked.

"I will never permit a row of medicine bottles to block my horizon," he replied.

Life can close in on us with brutal fury at times, but each of us always has the option to choose our own horizons.

TYING IT ALL TOGETHER

Tension is a fact of life. Whether it grinds us down or polishes us up depends upon how we handle the stress it generates. If we allow it to take charge of our lives it can grind us to powder, but if we grasp it firmly, we can subdue it and make it work *for* us to keep our lives interesting and challenging.

It takes constant vigilance and sometimes supreme effort to overrule the negative side of stress, but you can do it if you try.

Remember:

- You decide whether stress will be a helpful or hurtful force in your life.
- You can completely control what stress does to you.
- You can find all the resources you need to help you cope with whatever stress has done to you so far.
- You can use constructive stress as a powerful force to help you get more of what you want out of life.

THINK IT THROUGH

List the five most common causes of stress in your life and choose a primary strategy for dealing with each.

      STRESS SOURCE   COPING STRATEGY

1. _____   _____

2. _____   _____

3. _____   _____

4. _____   _____

5. _____   _____

ACTION STEP

Map out a complete strategy (based on what you've read in this chapter) for taking charge of stress in each area of your life. Set a definite time to help you implement your strategy.

CHAPTER ELEVEN

Life Is Better When You Live It *Up*

I saved the best for last for two big reasons.

First, it takes more than just having a good attitude to really become a high impact person. It takes knowing how to adapt to the relentless pressure of new situations, instead of always conforming to the expectations of others.

It also requires a full understanding and use of all of the strategies and skills we've explored so far—creative thinking, goal setting, time management and effective communication.

I hate books that say nothing more than "think positively and you'll get everything you want out of life." And, I suspect you hate them, too.

Yet, without a positive, upbeat attitude, none of the ideas in this book will work. It is the fundamental ingredient.

The second reason for saving this chapter for last is to challenge you to become a high impact person!

One of the most startling discoveries of my life was that I have the power to choose what kind of day I'm going to have. Each day arrives neutral—it's neither up nor down. I choose whether I will be up or down in that day.

The mood of my day is not set by my circumstances, by other people, by tasks I have to do, by events that happen along the way. It's set by only one thing—my attitude!

This is true for all of us. We may not always be able to control what happens to us, but we *can* always control the way we react to what happens.

Don't Conform—Adapt

We started this book by discussing the ways all of us are under constant pressure to conform, how the people around us have their own ideas about what we should do and what kinds of people we should be.

I shared with you my hope that you would resist that pressure to conform to the negative shaping and molding efforts of the subcultures you constantly find yourself in; that you would break out and become your own person.

The rest of the book has been designed to give you some practical ways to take charge of your own life and shape it as you see fit. We've explored what it means to choose your own goals, to plan your own life, to manage your own time and to impact positively on other people.

I think it only appropriate that we end the book by talking about how to choose the kind of mood you want your life to have.

I've tried it both ways. I've tried living life down—

feeling negative, rotten about myself, trying desperately to prove my self-worth to others. And, I've tried living life up—maintaining a positive mental attitude, accepting myself for who I am and boosting my self-esteem by achieving. Believe me, life is better when you live it up!

How do you stay positive in a negative world? Let me give you some pointers from the *Brooks Method* of self-motivation.

I. GETTING YOURSELF UP

"Bill, you really surprised me," a fellow said at the end of one of my time management seminars. "I thought you were going to step on my toes . . . instead you hit my starter button," he explained.

If I could do only one thing for you in this book, that's precisely what I'd choose to do—hit your starter button. I'd like to stimulate you to get started building the kind of life you want for yourself.

But, I realize that I can't motivate anyone. Only you can motivate yourself. In the final analysis, *all* motivation is self-motivation.

I hope you'll find these insights useful.

Insight 1:
An Up Day Starts The Night Before

The best time to ensure yourself of a good day is the night before. One reason many people are sick and tired of getting up every morning sick and tired, is that they always have such a lousy night. They focus on all the bad things that happened that day, they worry about what's going to happen tomorrow and they sleep in a bed full of anxieties.

I've found it helpful to spend some time each night reflecting on the good things that have happened that day. It's sometimes tough to get it started, but there is some good in the worst of days.

It's also helpful to lay out my clothes for the next day, check over my to do list, and plan something exciting to get my day started. I don't worry about tomorrow. I plan for it, then let it go.

John D. Rockefeller once told of how he ended each day. He said that he always emptied his pockets very slowly, the last thing before he retired. As he took things out of his pockets, he made a conscious effort to empty his mind of all worry, anxiety and negative thoughts. He didn't do badly for himself. Maybe it will work for you.

Insight 2:
The Most Important Hour Of The Day

The most important hour of each day is not the "happy hour" we hear so much about it—it's the first hour you're awake. That's what sets the pace for the whole day.

"The early morning hath gold in her mouth," said Ben Franklin.

If your day starts on a negative note, you can become filled with negative thoughts and ideas that hang around for the rest of the day. But starting out the day on a positive note sets a tone for positive thoughts all day. It's an emotional version of the law of inertia.

I strongly recommend that you start every day with a planned activity that you can feel good about; something that will almost certainly be successful. Don't leave it to be decided on the basis of what you feel like doing in the morning. You might feel like crawling back into bed. Plan specifically what you will do, and make sure it's something you will look forward to jumping into.

Insight 3:
Keep Your Goals In Sight

When Florence Chadwick set out from the coast of France to make her historic swim in 1952, she was full of hope and courage. The lone swimmer was surrounded by boats filled with journalists, well-wishers and a few skeptics. For years she had trained vigorously to build her stamina and disciplined her body to keep going long after everything within her cried out for her to quit.

As she neared the coast of England a heavy fog settled in and the waters became increasingly cold and choppy. "Come on Florence, you can make it!" her mother urged as she handed her some food. "It's only a few more miles! You're ahead of schedule!" But Florence was beaten by the tortuous elements of nature that day.

Exhausted, she finally asked to be pulled aboard the boat. She was heartbroken, especially when she discovered how close she'd come to her goal.

"I'm not making excuses," she later told reporters. "But I think I could have made it if I could only have seen my goal."

Florence determined to try again. This time, she added a new dimension to her daily training. She studied the shoreline of England where she expected to land, and memorized every feature of the seacoast. Each day as she swam, she would replay that mental image of her goal.

Eventually, she entered the waters again and set out for the coast of England. Along the way, she ran into all the fog, turbulence and cold water she'd met before. But this time something was different. She swam with greater vigor and determination. Even the skeptics noticed her new confidence.

She became the first woman in history to swim the English Channel.

What made the difference? She said later that it was because she was able to keep her goal clearly in focus in her mind, even when she couldn't see it with her eyes.

Your goals are only as secure as the vividness with which they are implanted in your mind. Visualize yourself reaching your goals and replay that mental picture. No matter what arises, you will be able to keep your sense of direction.

Insight 4:
Keep Building Yourself Up

Life will give you plenty of reasons for not feeling like doing the things you need to do to reach your goals. Your only real sources of inspiration to keep your motivation up are the reasons *you* create for doing what you must to succeed.

I have a friend who is a millionaire, and is often asked why he succeeded while others he grew up with never really made it. His simple answer is, "I guess I just had more reasons to get rich than they did."

A cartoon I once saw depicted a fellow riding in a cart behind a mule. He is holding a long pole out over the mule, with about a dozen carrots tied to it. The mule is stretched out in a dead run, and the caption reads, "If one carrot's good, maybe a bunch is better."

One of the best ways to keep yourself motivated is to develop as many reasons as you can to succeed, and to keep reminding yourself of all those reasons.

People can accomplish the most incredible things, if they have enough reasons!

Insight 5:
Play The Game To Win

Famous stock car driver Richard Petty tells a story about a lesson he learned from his mother after he'd come in second in his very first race.

"Son, you lost!" his mother said. "Richard, you don't have to run second to nobody!"

Young Richard got the message. For two decades he dominated the NASCAR circuit, and set records that are still standing.

Keep reminding yourself that you don't have to run second to anybody. To life's champions, it's never enough simply to be glad to be in the game—they're always in it to win it!

II. KEEPING YOURSELF UP

Barry Brown was one of the most promising young actors in Hollywood, according to leading movie critics, but you may not even remember him.

Bruce Brown, arts writer for the *Wall Street Journal*, calls Barry's story "one of the saddest stories ever to come out of Hollywood."

Barry was in movies such as "Bad Company" and "Daisy Miller," and was called by many critics "a young Jimmy Stewart."

As talented as he was, however, Barry kept getting

roles only in unsuccessful movies. Critics often cited his performance as a movie's "only saving grace." As a result, he found it increasingly hard to get work. Eventually, no one wanted to hire him.

He became depressed, started drinking heavily and behaving erratically. Finally, Barry Brown was found in his home, shot through the head. A gun and a bottle lay beside him.

Here was a young man who had talent, brains, looks and great potential. All he lacked was the one quality, the absence of which makes all other qualities useless—he lacked persistence.

A Different Scenario

Contrast that with the stories we've all heard about people who failed time and again, but ultimately succeeded. Babe Ruth held the record for strike-outs long before he set the record for home runs. Henry Ford forgot to put a reverse gear in his first car. Thomas Edison tried thousands of materials before he found the one that made his incandescent light work.

Many people who won only after repeated failures had mediocre talents. They struggled against overwhelming odds, and had many reasons to give up. But they all had the one quality Barry Brown lacked— they all had persistence.

I believe that persistence can be developed, even if you feel you were born without it. Most of us had it when we were children. We kept after what we wanted until we got it. But gradually, as we grew older, we began to rationalize ourselves right out of getting what we wanted. Eventually, disappointment didn't seem to matter to us so much anymore, and we found it easier and easier to give up.

How do you develop persistence?

Persistence Clue 1:
Winners Keep Getting Up

R. G. Le Tourneau, in his autobiography, told a story of failure after failure in his efforts to manufacture and sell his revolutionary new earth-moving machines and other radical ideas. He suffered one big disaster after another and went broke five times—each time just before he was about to make it big.

But Le Tourneau kept getting up and trying again. People who know heavy equipment tell me, virtually every giant earth mover you see at a road construction site was inspired by his designs.

You see, life's winners aren't the ones who are catapulted into fame and fortune. They're the people who fumble and fail over and over, who get knocked down time and again, but who always get back up and give it one more try.

And, what inspires me about them; they have a humility about them that can only be developed by struggle.

Persistence Clue 2:
Focus On Results—Not on Problems

"We've tried 20,000 experiments, and none of them have worked!" lamented Thomas Edison's lab assistant. "We don't know any more than we did when we started!"

They had been searching for a metal, or other substance, that would give off a brilliant glow when heated with electricity—a filament for the incandescent light bulb.

"Ah! But, yes!" Edison replied triumphantly. "We now know 20,000 substances that won't work!"

Losers talk about their problems, but winners talk about their results.

Persistence Clue 3:
Keep The Fire Burning

"You know you're getting old when you have more memories than dreams," someone said. If that's true, I've met a lot of thirty-year-old people who have been old a long time.

Wilma Rudolph looked out a hospital window and saw a stately mansion across the street. She was a little girl who'd been born prematurely, had nearly died twice from pneumonia and scarlet fever, and finally had been crippled by polio. Night after night she dreamed that she would one day live in a big house like that, and be able to run and play like the other children she knew.

The doctors didn't give her any hope that she'd ever even be able to walk—much less run.

"Mama," she said one night, "someday, I'm going to leave this town and make my place in the world."

"Honey, the most important thing in the world is for you to keep believing that," replied her mother, fighting hard to hold back the tears.

And Wilma did keep believing it. Through years of struggles that would make most of our complaints seem like nothing, she fought the odds. That little girl, from a poor family in Tennessee, would sneak around and pull off her brace when her parents were gone. She learned to walk when the doctors said it couldn't be done. She learned to run when her friends said there was no hope. She became a world class athlete when her coach laughed at the very idea.

In 1960, Wilma Rudolph stepped into a stadium

in Rome for the Olympic Games and 80,000 fans began chanting "Wilma! Wilma! Wilma!"

After a modest wave to silence the crowd, she posted three record-setting races, and became the first woman in history to win three gold medals!

What gave her the persistence to keep going under such overwhelming odds? She kept the fire burning!

THERE'S MORE TO YOU THAN YOU'VE THOUGHT

That little voice way down inside you that keeps whispering "There's more to you than you've thought!" is right.

Arnold Lemerand was taking a leisurely stroll, on Saturday, November 1, 1980, when he saw a small child pinned beneath an 1800-pound clay pipe on a construction site. Lemerand, age 56, looked around for someone to help but there was no one. Realizing that the boy would soon die unless rescued, he did the only thing he could do—he reached down and lifted the huge pipe off the little fellow's head. When he tried to lift that pipe later he could not budge it.

You never know what you can do until you have to do something that is beyond all the limits you have previously set for yourself. At that moment, you will discover the tremendous power of your own desire.

Maybe you don't particularly want to lift an 1800-pound pipe. It's not the sort of thing most people do for kicks. I would bet there is something you would really love to do, if you had the resources. I'd also bet you could come a lot closer than you might think, if you could find a way to tap that inner-reserve all of us have deep inside us.

Perhaps you've got a song or a book to write, or a corporation to start or a product to invent. Maybe you've backed away from it because you've bought into the notion of your subcultures that you don't quite have what it takes.

History is full of stories of people who did what everyone around them thought was impossible. They did it because they connected with an inner power that comes only from a burning desire.

Why not start tapping into some of that power, right now? It begins when you decide to adapt and make the most of your life, instead of conforming to the world around you.

Good luck! I hope you get everything you want out of life!

ABOUT THE AUTHOR

Bill Brooks is a nationally known professional speaker, sales and personal development specialist whose clients include Chevrolet, IBM, Metropolitan Life, U.S. Steel, Lockheed and scores of others. He is the owner and president of two successful companies: William T. Brooks and Associates, which specializes in seminars, consulting services to major corporations and motivational training; and Developmental Learning Systems, which creates and distributes innovative educational products and systems. Bill is an honors graduate of Gettysburg College with a masters degree from Syracuse University. He is a former college football coach, award winning sales professional and university administrator. Bill lives in Greensboro, North Carolina with his wife, Nancy, and their two sons, Will and Jeb.